OTHER BOOKS BY DEBRA K. FARRINGTON

Hearing with the Heart
Learning to Hear with the Heart

Living Faith Day by Day
Unceasing Prayer
One Like Jesus
Romancing the Holy

THE SEASONS OF A RESTLESS HEART

A Spiritual Companion for
Living in Transition

DEBRA K. FARRINGTON

JOSSEY-BASS
A Wiley Imprint
www.josseybass.com

Published by Jossey-Bass

A Wiley Imprint

989 Market Street, San Francisco, CA 94103-1741   www.josseybass.com

Credits are on page 180.

Jossey-Bass books and products are available through most bookstores. To contact Jossey-Bass directly call our Customer Care Department within the U.S. at 800-956-7739, outside the U.S. at 317-572-3986, or fax 317-572-4002.

Jossey-Bass also publishes its books in a variety of electronic formats. Some content that appears in print may not be available in electronic books.

Library of Congress Cataloging-in-Publication Data

Farrington, Debra K.

  The seasons of a restless heart: a spiritual companion for living in transition /
Debra K. Farrington.—1st ed.

    p. cm.

  Includes bibliographical references.

  ISBN 0–7879–7392–0 (alk. paper)

  1. Spiritual life—Christianity. I. Title.

  BV4501.3.F375 2005

  248.4—dc22   2004022756

Printed in the United States of America

FIRST EDITION

HB Printing   10 9 8 7 6 5 4 3 2 1

Contents

ACKNOWLEDGMENTS   ix

Introduction   1

I   The Restless Season   5

II   Restlessness and Creativity   23

III   Help!   45

IV   Eat, Sleep, Bend, and Stretch   67

V   Are We There Yet?   97

VI   You Put Your Right Foot In,
You Put Your Right Foot Out   121

VII   Home Again   141

RESOURCES   159

NOTES   161

THE AUTHOR   167

v

Blessed be the Lord!
for he has shown me the wonders
of his love in a besieged city.
—Psalm 31:21

For Marley, and in loving memory of Codi,
both of whom have made many important transitions with me

Acknowledgments

In the midst of thinking about and writing this book, the joke seemed to be on me. I went through one transition after another. I was diagnosed with multiple sclerosis and learned to make all the adjustments to life that requires. I found a house I wasn't looking for, bought it, and moved into it—an eighty-year-old house that needs lots of tender-loving care. My beloved cat, Codi, developed renal failure and died. In my more cynical moments, it seemed as if the Holy Spirit, with either an outrageous sense of humor or what seemed like just plain meanness, was making sure that I'd write an honest book, not a sugar-coated or Pollyanna one. In the moments when I sense my connection to that Spirit, I recognize her not as a nemesis but as a helper, though I reserve the right to believe that she plays rough at times!

Throughout the writing of this book, there were many who, either prompted by the Spirit or out of their own gracious and loving hearts, helped me through the transitions and encouraged me when the writing was tough. My editor, Sheryl Fullerton, is a godsend, with a great eye and the ability to be both absolutely honest and tactful at the same time. She is what a writer-friend of mine called a "nonanxious presence," which is a great gift and one that

I will continue trying to emulate in my own personal and professional life. My agent, Linda Roghaar, has believed in this project since it first started talking to me seven years ago, albeit in a far different form. Bless her for keeping the ancient book proposal I wrote (that no one wanted to publish for all those years!) until the idea of writing a book on "living in transition" matured. I am so grateful for her interest in my work and for her unwavering support and patience.

In any publishing project there are also people behind the scenes whose work improves a manuscript or makes it look marvelous. They're the unsung heroes of book publishing! So let me sing the praises of Mary O'Briant, the marvelous copyeditor; Paula Goldstein, who designed the cover and pages of this book, and the mistress of production behind all of it, Joanne Clapp Fullagar, whom I treasure not only for her technical skills, but for her quick wit and friendship.

I also owe a great deal to the gracious and gentle people who read various drafts of the manuscript and contributed their expertise to it: Mary Earle and Anne Kitch—fine priests, friends, and fellow writers—and Carla Pineda, Nancy Artz, and Deb Roth, who were kind enough to read this book as they were going through their own major transitions. Gifted author and friend Susan Jorgensen helped guide me out of confusion with the book at a particularly crucial point, and I am deeply grateful.

Finally, I am grateful to Marley, who not only gave up many weekends, when we could have been out in the world doing something fun, so I could sit in my office and write, but who also helped me clarify some very muddled thinking at important junctures. He has a good eye, a keen mind, and one of the most loving hearts I've ever encountered.

THE SEASONS
OF A
RESTLESS HEART

Introduction

"Creation takes a lot longer than destruction," said our tour guide, a park ranger for Glacier Bay National Park. She didn't mean it as a theological statement. She was talking about what happens in nature when ice recedes from the glaciers and leaves barren rock on which new life might develop. But her statement stuck with me. It spoke to me about my own life. Creation has always taken way too long for someone as impatient as I can be, while destruction—losses, changes, shifts—seems to happen too often and too unexpectedly.

Not all changes in life happen instantly. A relationship may have been changing and dissolving over several months or years. A loved one might have been ill for a long time, or we might notice we're aging and not as healthy as we once were. A child grows up, gradually detaching herself from her parents as she becomes her own person. But finally, at some point, the relationship ends, the loved one dies, the diagnosis of illness comes, or the child goes off to college. And the changes that have been slowly creeping up on us arrive in earnest. We are in transition.

Probably transition has been going on for quite a while already, but it wasn't recognized or admitted. More often than not, the challenge of living into that transition looks onerous. But transitions, both those we initiated and those we didn't, are a part of the life cycle, a part of growth. Like it or not, in the midst of transition, the work is going to be about creation, about cooperating with God in re-creating ourselves, about becoming more fully what God calls us to be.

That was the work of the Israelites in the Exodus story in the Bible as well. Their stories, with all of the danger, frustration, and restlessness, speak powerfully to me in the midst of my own transitions. As slaves in Egypt, they lived hard lives. They worked long hours in difficult conditions. They were treated harshly by their overlords and given fewer resources than they needed for doing their work. Then along came Moses, who freed the people of Israel from slavery. He led them out of Egypt and into the desert, on a journey that was longer (forty years!) and more difficult than any of them expected. They didn't like the transition process one bit, not any more than I do. They wanted to go from being slaves to being the free people of God in a day, or perhaps a week. But it took a lot longer than that for them to be re-created. It takes all of us a lot longer than we'd like as well. That is the nature of transitions.

The process for the Israelites and for us resembles the process of glaciers becoming whole new environments—a lesson I learned from the park ranger I mentioned earlier. When ice recedes from glaciers, it leaves barren rock on which nothing is growing and not much seems to be happening. But if the rock is porous—and that's critical—water, wind, and birds will bring organic matter and drop it into the crevices. Those crevices give the materials a safe place to lodge and take hold, and, over time, with appropriate water and sun, plants begins to grow. Small plants come first—lichen and moss and other sorts of ground cover. As they take hold, somewhat larger plants begin to grow. Shrubs can send down roots, and there is enough ground cover to hold them fast while the shrubs grow larger. Cottonwood trees come next, and finally the spruces have enough soil and nutrients to grow in. If that process is rushed—if a plant tries to jump into the cycle before its time—it is liable to die. Spruces had come into a part of the park too early, our guide told us, and beetles were killing them. Trying to grow before their time—before their place was ready—meant that they lacked the necessary nutrients and immunity from the bugs that they should have had.

Transitions share a lot in common with the way life changes and develops on glaciated rock. Transitions happen in their own time and in their own way, and trying to rush through them can sabotage the whole effort. Most of us know this at some level, but we still want to push the process and control the outcome. We're like the man who tried to rid his lawn of dandelions. He tried everything he knew of to stop the dandelions from growing on his otherwise beautiful lawn. Finally, in desperation he wrote the Department of Agriculture and begged for a solution. He so wanted a perfect lawn, green and smooth and flawless. But the answer he got back wasn't the one he wanted: "We suggest you learn to love the dandelions," they wrote. Learning to love the dandelions is what the transition process is all about. It's only when we learn to love them that we'll find our way forward.

But that seems like a chore that's forced on us because there's no other choice. A transition feels the same way—like an endurance contest that would be better if it would end sooner rather than later. I can't honestly deny that there are days—many of them—when I see transitions that way, too. They're enough to make you question the existence of a loving God sometimes. Still I'd like to invite you to think of transitions a little differently as you read this book. Like the Department of Agriculture officials in the story, I want to invite you to *actually* learn to love the dandelions.

If doing it out of a sense of duty or resignation is the starting place for you, that's fine. If that's all you can manage for the moment, then just do it because you think you ought to. But I hope to provide some perspectives here that will help you see that the dandelion—the transition you're living in—has a beauty of its own. Like other plants, it has a season as well. Dandelions come in the early spring in my part of the country, and then they're gone a month or so later.

Transitions come and go in the same way, though they don't usually disappear so quickly. Finding ways to befriend them, to actually love the process, even if only a little bit, not only makes the journey easier but we stand a better chance of being closer to God when we reach the end.

CHAPTER I

The Restless Season

For everything there is a season,
and a time for every matter under heaven:
a time to be born, and a time to die; a time to plant,
and a time to pluck up what is planted;
a time to kill, and a time to heal;
a time to break down, and a time to build up;
a time to weep, and a time to laugh;
a time to mourn, and a time to dance;
a time to throw away stones, and a time to gather
stones together; a time to embrace,
and a time to refrain from embracing;
a time to seek, and a time to lose; a time to keep,
and a time to throw away;
a time to tear, and a time to sew;
a time to keep silence, and a time to speak;
a time to love, and a time to hate; a time for war,
and a time for peace.
—ECCLESIASTES 3:1–8

As the sage of Ecclesiastes said, there is, indeed, a time for everything. But chances are that if you've picked up this book, the time you find yourself in is one of transition. Divorce, loss of a job, an empty nest, a move across the country, loss of a loved one, a chronic illness, and any number of other transitions all share something in common: they dump us—sometimes rather unceremoniously—flat into an unsettled time, a restless season.

After dealing with the shock and the overwhelming grief, after friends and family have stopped asking so often how you are, when you find yourself someplace that feels unfamiliar, that's the beginning of a journey in what often feels like desert space—a time when the heart is restless and unsettled, when the empty horizon seems to stretch out endlessly, leading nowhere, and resources seem scarce.

In my own times of transition, I've found that there are lots of resources for dealing with the initial shock or movement or sorrow that begins a transitional time in life. That doesn't make the time any easier, nor do all those resources make living through the time any easier. It doesn't even seem to matter whether the transition is forced on us or we choose it. In all cases, something happens to bring about an ending in our life—one that forces us to reevaluate and probably to grow in some new direction. When those transitions hit, friends and loved ones are often willing to stay with us and help. Colleagues and those around us know that something is wrong, and the world, in general, tends to cut us a little slack. William Bridges, the author of the popular and helpful book, *Transitions*,[1] calls this first stage "the ending." The final stage of his three-step exploration of transitions is "the new beginning"—the time, way down the road, when we've figured out where we want to head or feel compelled to go.

In between the ending and the beginning is a long stretch of time, often the most difficult piece of the journey. Bridges dubs this "neutral time"; I find it anything but that. The word *neutral* implies that not a whole lot is happening, and although decisions aren't being made quickly and not much gets resolved from day to day, all kinds of things are happening. To me, transitions are more like the time the Israelites spent wandering in the desert—empty, extreme in its emotional temperatures, confusing to navigate, and hard to wait out. They're also unavoidable. There's no such thing as a quick and easy transition from the shock of some change that we seek or that is thrust upon us and whatever new beginning lies ahead. Just as the cold of the winter months creates conditions that help spring flowers bloom gloriously, so the conditions of time spent in the desert work their way into the soul and, if we let them, the time spent there brings forth new life.

The restlessness of transitions, though it feels lousy—even outright crushing—at times, is like the growing pains of adolescence. It's a sign that the heart and mind and soul are alive and kicking, looking for more, asking questions. This time between the first stages of grief or mourning and the discovery of Canaan—the place to which God guides us—is far from neutral. It's more than an endurance contest. Often it's lonely or frustrating, or both. Anthropologists call it "liminal time"—the kind of time between one stage of life and the next. In some cultures, for instance, boys go out into the wilderness by themselves on a vision quest or some other established ritual, and when they come back they are now considered to be men. That time in the wilderness is liminal time—the time between here and there, when we're not really sure anymore who or where we are or where we're going. Desert time is painful, but it's also alive with creative potential.

The story is told of Henry Ford, the founder of the first American automobile-manufacturing company, who hired an efficiency expert to go through his plant and make recommendations about improving operations. The efficiency expert found that the factory worked pretty well and had high praise for Ford, except in one area. There was, apparently, a man who routinely sat with his feet up on his desk, thinking. The efficiency expert thought the man was wasting time, but Ford promptly corrected him. "That man once had an idea that earned us a fortune. At the time, I believe his feet were exactly where they are now."[2] In the middle stage of transition it often looks as if we are doing nothing; sometimes it even feels as if we're doing nothing. But the reality is that creative stuff is happening, and what we have to do during this time is to settle into the nothingness and see what comes of all of it.

> *O Lord Jesus Christ, who art the Way, the Truth, and the Life, we pray Thee suffer us not to stray from Thee who are the Way; nor to distrust Thee who are the Truth, nor to rest in any other thing than Thee, who are the Life. Teach us by the Holy Spirit what to believe, what to do, and where to take our rest. We ask it for Thy own name's sake.*
>
> —ERASMUS

Does that mean that God inflicts change on us to force growth? Is this some cosmic version of tough love? I don't think so. I'm willing to acknowledge, along with Job, that I wasn't there when God created everything and that I don't really know how or why things work as they do. There are some mysteries in this life, like the Divine Mystery Itself, which I call God, that I don't expect to understand on this side of the grave, at least not completely. But that said, my sense is that God calls me beloved, and the One who loves me does not wish misery on me. That One who loves me loves you, too, and has no desire to see you suffer either.

But stuff happens in this world. Germs and genes leave people ill, sometimes deathly ill. Human affections shift or change over time and disrupt relationships. Companies transfer workers, or we choose to move to far-flung parts of the country or the world and communities get disrupted. People and nations declare war on one another and find all kinds of other ways to hurt each other. Earthquakes, floods, and hurricanes do their damage.

Good stuff happens, too. Children are born, bringing great changes into their parents' lives. Graduations propel people forward. Two people who love one another get married. Someone gets a promotion. Spring comes again each year, and flowers start bursting out all over. God watches all of this and uses whatever happens as an invitation to us to co-create with him.[3] God has hopes and desires for this world, and for each of us, but they're just that—hopes and desires, not edicts. God watches all that happens and celebrates or weeps with us, as the situation demands, but the Holy One has also given us free will and respects the decisions we feel compelled to make. God helps us find the way forward, whatever happens.

In a marvelous book, *The Hopeful Heart,* priest and writer John Claypool explores the three ways that God, who loves us deeply, gives us the hope we need to help us move forward. The first is that sometimes God provides a miracle, which isn't as far-fetched or unusual as we like to think, says Claypool. The fact that we were born at all, that we continue to walk and breathe on this earth day after day, is a miracle in and of itself. The third way that God works with us is to give us the gift of endurance, the ability to bear whatever we must bear for as long as necessary. But this book focuses on Claypool's second way that God provides us with graceful help. The second is that God collaborates with us. As Claypool says, "God moves alongside us and invites us to join forces with him in bringing about a solution to our difficulties. Our identity as co-creators becomes a reality when this happens. We are offered the opportunity of combining our skills, insights, and energies with those of God to resolve our problems."[4] In the midst of transition, God invites us to listen to our hearts and attend to God's movements—to collaborate as we find our way forward in life.

There are times in the midst of any transition when we're too tired, too weary, or too weak to participate in the collaborative process, or when it's just not time for our active participation. In the early stages of labor, for instance, a woman has to breathe through the contractions and wait until it is time for her to do something more. That's not to say that the breathing and waiting, and resisting doing anything else, isn't hard work. It is! The Israelites in the desert found it most difficult to just wait and breathe and avoid pushing. But this is the time for trusting that God holds us and guides us, and to rest, as much as possible, in that knowledge.

 Holy God, loving Father, of the world everlasting,

Grant me to have of Thee this living prayer;

Lighten my understanding, kindle my will, begin my doing,

Incite my love, strengthen my weakness, enfold my desire.

—ALEXANDER CARMICHAEL

But there comes a time, and in labor it is called "the transition," when it is time to push, to get very involved in moving the process forward. There is a stage in the midst of most journeys when we have the energy, the alertness, the desire, when our hearts are so restless that we're ready to be involved in the conversation and the choices, when there is energy enough to recognize that God wants to collaborate with us and to begin to listen and respond. It is my deepest hope that this book will help you become more aware of those opportunities and find ways to respond instead of experiencing the desert as an endurance contest and nothing more.

"Look well to the growing edge!" counsels twentieth-century priest and writer Howard Thurman in his poem, "The Growing Edge."

> *All around us worlds are dying and new worlds are being*
> *born;*
> *All around us life is dying and life is being born:*
> *The fruit ripens on the tree;*
> *The roots are silently at work in the darkness of the earth*
> *Against the time when there shall be new leaves, fresh*
> *blossoms,*
> *green fruit.*
> *Such is the growing edge!*
> *It is the extra breath from the exhausted lung,*
> *The one more thing to try when all else has failed,*
> *The upward reach of life when weariness closes in upon all*
> *endeavor.*
> *This is the basis of hope in moments of despair,*
> *The incentive to carry on when times are out of joint*
> *And men have lost their reason; the source of confidence*
> *When worlds crash and dreams whiten into ash.*
> *The birth of a child—life's most dramatic answer to*
> *death—*
> *This is the Growing Edge incarnate,*
> *Look well to the growing edge!*[5]
> —Howard Thurman

"Looking to the growing edge" sounds nice, of course, but it is extraordinarily hard work. I don't know about you, but if my world should crash and my dreams whiten into ash, my first inclination would be one of great frustration, fear, and sorrow. I would not be jumping up and down for joy because I thought God was inviting me into something new. It's so important to do the work of grieving, which comes with all transitions, not just the unhappy ones. Even a new and exciting opportunity brings with it loss—loss of freedom, loss of good friends or community, radical changes in the schedule, and demands on one's life. Grieving the losses, even when there's something new to celebrate, but especially when the loss is the predominant theme in your life, is crucial, and it takes time. This isn't a book primarily about that grieving or mourning stage. This book is for the time after you've gotten past the initial shock of change, when you find yourself, as the Israelites did, on a long desert journey to a place you can't yet name. Looking for the growing edge is an activity best engaged in while walking the desert's long stretches of hot, dry sand, rather than in the midst of deep grieving. Like the lichen and shrubs and spruce, everything has to grow in its own time.

The transition process is a little like a story that Catholic priest and collector of stories Anthony De Mello tells about an unnamed man:

> He was becoming blind by degrees. He fought it with every means in his power. When medicine no longer served to fight it, he fought it with his emotions. It took courage to say to him, "I suggest you learn to love your blindness."
>
> It was a struggle. He refused to have anything to do with it in the beginning. And when he eventually brought himself to speak to his blindness his words were bitter. But he kept on speaking and the words slowly changed into words of resignation and tolerance and acceptance . . . and, one

day, very much to his own surprise, they became words of friendliness . . . and love. Then came the day when he was able to put his arm around his blindness and say, "I love you." That was the day I saw him smile again.[6]

This book is a guide to the journey that begins when you reach the place where, like the blind man, you are ready to start talking to your transition, even if all you have to offer are bitter words. As De Mello's story highlights, you can bring whatever emotions you're feeling along with you on the journey. It doesn't matter if you're headed into the desert angry, resigned, frightened, or full of other emotions. God understands, accepts, and can work with whatever you're carrying around with you right now. Start from where you are, not from where you're not.

∿ Following Your Heart ∿

One of the Desert Fathers (men who lived devout monastic lives in the desert in the third and fourth centuries after Christ) told the story of a man who wanted to know how he should live.

> A brother questioned an old man saying, "What good work should I do so that I may live?" The old man said, "God knows what is good. I have heard it said that one of the Fathers asked Abba Nisterus the Great, the friend of Abba Antnony, and said to him, 'What good work is there that I could do?' He said to him, "Are not all actions equal? Scripture says that Abraham was hospitable and God was with him. David was humble, and God was with him. Elias loved interior peace and God was with him. So, do whatever you see your soul desires according to God and guard your heart."[7]

Though it can be hard to hear what your soul is trying to tell you while you're in transition, especially at its most restless and arid, the work of the desert time is learning to listen to your heart. That's what I hope we can explore together in this book. This is the time to let your heart's desires speak to you—not completely unfettered, of course. I'll talk about some safeguards to employ when you seek to listen to what your heart is saying. But more often than not, people fail to listen to what their hearts most deeply desire. Those messages from the heart get dismissed as fanciful, impractical, or impossible. But it is through the heart that God often speaks to us and invites us on the journey that will eventually bring us to Canaan.

Jesus, confirm my heart's desire

To work, and speak, and think for Thee;

Still let me guard the holy fire

And stir up Thy gift in me.

—CHARLES WESLEY

For the ancient Hebrew people, the heart was something more than just a physical organ of the body. The heart was the place from which everything important emanated. Physical health, emotions, spirituality, and intellect all began in the heart. A *restless heart,* using the ancient Hebrew sense of the word, then, means that all aspects of our being feel restless. We experience that restlessness physically, emotionally, spiritually, and even intellectually in the midst of transition, just as the Israelites did in the ancient stories that fill Exodus, Numbers, Leviticus, and Deuteronomy. And like the Israelites, we want the restlessness—the discomforts of the desert—to end, sooner rather than later. The work of transition is about learning to listen patiently to the restlessness in our hearts—our bodies, minds, and souls—and to live with it long enough to get to know its name, and to discover if, through it, God is inviting us to some kind of promised land.

It is this understanding of the heart, as the whole of our being, that leaves me with anxiety about some of the language used to explain the process of leaving behind some aspect of life and moving into a new one. Various writers—be they spiritual leaders, psychologists, or others—talk about the need to (at best) leave behind and (at worst) kill off the old or false self. I struggle with the idea that there *is* an old or false self. We may have a self or self-image that is culturally conditioned, as some have said,[8] but I have a hard time believing that the self I was years ago, before some important changes in my life, was a false one. It was the self I needed to be at that time, and God loved me just as I was. It is more helpful, I find, to think of myself as someone who is becoming more and more of what God hopes and desires for me as I learn to listen more deeply, and as I become more willing to be open to God's transforming love. That doesn't make the younger Debra false, just less developed. And the experiences of those earlier years were important. They taught me key lessons and helped me learn to see and hear with my heart today. God willing, the experiences of the person I am now will do the same for the person I am becoming.

God be in my head,
and in my understanding.
God be in my eyes,
and in my looking;
God be in my mouth,
and in my speaking;
God be in my heart,
and in my thinking.

ANONYMOUS (C. 1514)

The whole issue of "dying to ourselves" in the process of growing in Christian faith and in living through transitional times also deserves careful questioning. Contemporary scholars have begun to understand that this particular image may be more helpful to some than to others who seek to grow in loving God. The image of "dying to self," for instance, may be far more helpful to men than to women. "Not only is psychology affected by a male bias, but also religion," write the authors of *Healing the Eight Stages of Life.*

> Many assumptions are based on male experience. For example, men who have been raised to compete with and dominate others may understandably perceive sin as pride. This male view of sin as pride has become central to Christian spirituality; the remedy is seen as "dying to self."[9]

Many women, on the other hand, have been raised to put the needs of others before their own and to ignore their own deepest desires. Asking them to die to those desires and needs even more proves enormously detrimental, impeding spiritual growth and connection with God.

More male-biased language fills the pages of the Bible. In the story of the Israelites' transition from Egypt to Canaan, the people stubbornly refuse to enter Canaan the first time they get there, and God condemns them to wander in the desert for forty more years until the generation that defied God has died. It's pretty simple to translate that story as being about killing off the old self or (more passively) letting the old self die so that the newer, truer self can enter Canaan. And if that language works for you and helps you understand how to get through desert times, then go ahead and use it.

But if that kind of language gets in your way and makes you want to give up altogether, here's different imagery. The journey for the Israelites was about learning how to stop being slaves and become, more fully, the people of God. Journeys through desert times are similar: they require that we move from being wherever we are today to a place of even deeper connection with God. That doesn't necessarily involve leaving behind every aspect of who we have been. Rather, it is about the transformation of what we have been into what we will be, much as the caterpillar transforms into a butterfly. As Sue Monk Kidd, contemporary spirituality writer and novelist, writes:

> The life of the spirit is never static. We're born on one level, only to find some new struggle toward wholeness gestating within. That's the sacred intent of life, of God—to move us continuously toward growth, toward recovering all that is lost and orphaned within us and restoring the divine image imprinted on our soul. And rarely do significant shifts come without a sense of our being lost in dark woods. . . . [10]

Kidd's words—"a sense of our being lost"—are important. We have the sense that we are lost many times, but God hasn't lost track of us. God has hopes and desires for us and knows where we are at any point in time. The hard part for us is trusting that eventually we'll get a sense of God's guidance so that we no longer feel quite so lost.

Learning to trust in God's ongoing guidance is a little like the story of the atheist who fell off a cliff but managed to catch hold of a small branch that kept him from falling to his death. Not knowing what else to do, he shouted for God. No answer. He shouted again: "God, if you actually exist, save me, and I'll tell everyone else about you." At first all he heard was more silence, but then a voice from the heavens said quietly: "That's what they all say when they need my help." The atheist protested: "I really mean it, God. I believe in you now. Just save me and you'll see what good I'll do in your name." God agreed to save the man. "Just let go of the branch, and I'll save you," God replied. "You must be out of your mind," shouted the man. "Save me without my having to let go of this branch."

O supreme and unapproachable light! O whole and blessed truth. How far you are from me, who am so near to you! Everywhere you are wholly present, yet I do not see you. In you I move, and in you I have my being, and cannot come to you; you are within me, and around me, and I do not feel you.

—ANSELM

God does guide our transitions but not always the way we have in mind. We sometimes even think this guidance is crazy or impossible. The stories found in Exodus, Numbers, and Deuteronomy are full of people who alternately clung to God and thought God crazy or irrational, and those stories form a backdrop to this book. More often than not, those stories are held up as ones about the Israelites' (and ours, by extension) obedience and disobedience to God's law, and there's a lot to say about that in those narratives. But they are also stories about the difficulty of living in transition—the in-between times.

In the Israelites' struggle to live in the desert without knowing where they were headed, when they would get there, and what the new land would be like, I see my own struggles with transitional times. It's not hard to identify with their frustrations and their pigheadedness. The stories found in these scriptures are stories about God's continuing efforts to grow the people out of slavery and into their identity as people of God. In much the same way, without the same particulars, our own transitions are always about becoming more deeply the person God sees in us. And so the

Clothe me, clothe me with yourself, eternal truth, so that I may live this early life with true obedience, and with the light of your most holy faith.

—CATHERINE OF SIENA

stories of the Israelites and their long journey from Egypt to Canaan are our stories as well. If you haven't read Exodus, Numbers, and Deuteronomy recently, you may well find a quick review of them enlightening.

In using these narratives as part of this book's backbone, however, I need to remind you and myself that these stories aren't blueprints for living in transition. They weren't written to be a "transition manual" and can't be read as self-help books. The stories found there are enormously instructive and even comforting for those who are exploring the restlessness of desert times, but the stories can be stretched too thin in trying to make them fit the transitions in the lives of twenty-first-century people.

In the pages that follow, I offer suggestions based on my own studies and experiences about understanding transitions as creative processes rather than endurance contests. There are so many different kinds of transitions, and we each come to them with different expectations and needs, so not everything in the following chapters will be useful to all people at all times. I've included a variety of spiritual practices to help you explore some of the ideas in the book, as well as prayers that speak to the issues you may be facing. Use what's helpful to you in the midst of your own transition, and don't worry about trying to use everything in the book. Pay attention as well to suggestions that seem to call to you and to ideas that really bother you. Sometimes the very things that frighten or repel are just what we need to pay attention to at the moment. But use your own good sense in deciding what, from all the material in this book, is helpful to you in the midst of your particular transition.

∾ Praying and Journaling in the Desert ∾

When I am writing a book—a process that has a lot in common with transitions—I find it helpful to keep a journal of my thoughts. I recommend that you keep a transitions journal as you travel through your own desert. The journal isn't a diary in the traditional sense. There are no rules about how often to write or what to put in it. Keeping a journal is just a way to record random thoughts, musings, hopes, miseries, desires, or anything else that comes to you. The journal I've kept while writing this book is full of random ideas, written down as they came to me. I didn't end up using all of them, but it was fascinating to review what I'd written over eighteen months as I was finishing the book. I discovered thoughts I'd lost track of, some of which were still important and others that seemed less so. A transition journal of your own will help you in the same way and give you something to look back at, as you gain some perspective on the journey you're embarked on.

Any kind of journal will do, but I'd recommend one that is easy to write in. Something spiral-bound, or one that lays flat without your having to hold it down forcibly is best. There are lots of decorative and expressive journals on the market, and you may find the perfect one for you. The journal that seemed to find me as I contemplated this book had a wonderful quote about growing more like ourselves as we grow older, and the journal practically jumped into my hands as the perfect one for this book. If you can't find one that suits you, create your own. Decorate it however it suits you, using crayons or paints, fabric, or whatever you like. This is your journal, your companion for the journey; throughout the book, I'll make suggestions about things to think about and record in it. Use the exercises if you find them helpful, but don't limit yourself to my suggestions. Write anything that seems pertinent to you in your transitions journal. You never know what thoughts and ideas will rise to the surface as you travel along.

This book is also full of prayers that may be helpful along the way. In the midst of transition, sometimes the words we need just won't come. There are times, many of them, when just sitting quietly with God, saying nothing, is just exactly what you'll need to do, and far be it from me to ever discourage anyone from just sitting companionably with God. It's some of the best medicine I know. But if you're searching for words and can't find ones of your own that seem to fit, I've included a selection of prayers that speak to the fears, joys, and restlessness of transitional times.

Praying often comes naturally during transitions. In good times, it's easy to forget about God, but when the path is difficult we're more aware of wanting and needing God's presence. Try to take time for prayer on a regular basis, even if it's just a few minutes a day. Your prayers don't have to be complicated. Just talk to God, and don't worry about whether or not your prayers sound well-put-together or elegant. God doesn't care about that. Just communicate with God in any way that works

God, my Source of Strength:

A season is turning in my life

Calling me to make ready:

Walk with me, I pray.

This unmapped course lies divided ahead

Urging careful determination:

Walk with me, I pray.

The gate has swung open and everything's loose

Bidding that someone be left behind:

Walk with me, I pray.

Until the turbulent waters clear

I reach for your mercy

And pray for wisdom:

Walk with me, I pray.[11]

—KERI WEHLANDER

best for you. It may be sitting quietly for a while. Or taking a walk and letting your mind and heart pray and listen. Gardening, cleaning the house, or anything else that helps you clear your mind to talk with God and to listen is great. Pay attention to any resistance you have to praying during this time of transition. See if you can decipher what that's about, and use your journal to reflect on your experience.

Prayer isn't magic. It won't always be comforting to pray, though it's unlikely that it will never offer comfort. Prayer isn't about convincing God to do what you want the Holy One to do. It's about talking through your restlessness, your fears, your joys, and your hopes, and listening for God's response. And in the midst of transition, it is often about simply learning to seek God's guidance, even in the dark.

CHAPTER II

Restlessness and Creativity

*Crisis, change, all the myriad upheavals that blister
the spirit and leave us groping—they aren't voices
simply of pain but also of creativity.*[1]
—SUE MONK KIDD

Once when I was considering becoming self-employed, I read a self-help book that told me exactly how to navigate the process. It detailed the decisions and preparations I needed to make and the lifestyle changes—financial, emotional, and otherwise—I should expect. The author presented just the right blend of reality about the difficulties and joys of being self-employed, along with solid warnings and encouragement. Anyone, on finishing that book, would feel equipped to move forward in the process, captain of her own ship. And although that's a great feeling, and self-help books are meant to leave readers with those encouraged feelings, no book (this one included!) can take away the sheer difficulty of doing something new or differently.

That's especially true for transitions. They're messy and difficult. And we're not even in control of so many aspects, no matter what self-help books or our own egos try to tell us. In so many transitions, parts or all of the decisions or desired results lie outside our own hands.

It's not hard to see why that's the case. Many transitions aren't planned. Moses certainly wasn't planning to go back to Egypt, much less to become the leader of the Israelites. The spouse who gets asked for a divorce, the relationship that ends suddenly, the unexpected death of a loved one, an earthquake or fire that destroys a home—none of those can be anticipated or orchestrated. They're simply thrust upon us. Even when a transition is planned and managed, like a change of jobs or graduation from college, surprises still seem to spring from nowhere. Transitions are full of messiness. They're often frustrating at best and painful at their worst. In some ways, I wouldn't wish a transition on my best friend.

But then again, I guess I would. Transitions, despite their discomfort, are opportunities for creativity, chances to open up to something new. If I were going to recommend a slogan for people in transition, I'd say the prophet Isaiah has it perfectly: "I am about to do a new thing; now it springs forth, do you not perceive it?"

The sheer unmanageability of transition also helps us remember something we tend to forget when times are easy: God is our partner in this creativity. No one flies solo, at least not successfully and not forever. God needs our attention and cooperation in transition, and we need God to help us create a new future. "We are . . . called to share with God the work of *creating* the truth of our identity," [italics in original text] wrote Trappist monk Thomas Merton. "We can evade this responsibility by playing with masks, and this pleases us because it can appear at times to be a free and creative way of living. . . . But in the long run the cost and the sorrow come very high."[2] Trying to control our own destiny, to pull ourselves up by our own bootstraps without God's help, can be very costly. Or it can fail completely, as the Israelites found out time after time in the desert.

That doesn't mean, however, that God has already created an identity or plan we have to guess and then follow. In

Almighty and everlasting God, you made the universe with all its marvelous order, its atoms, worlds, and galaxies, and the infinite complexity of living creatures: Grant that, as we probe the mysteries of your creation, we may come to know you more truly, and more surely fulfill our role in your eternal purpose; in the name of Jesus Christ our Lord. Amen.

—THE BOOK OF
COMMON PRAYER
1979

workshops and classes I've led on discerning God's desires for our lives, many participants seem to think that God has one blueprint for each of our lives, and our job is to figure out what that blueprint is and to follow it. But God's action in human life is really more resonant of the story about the pilgrim who walked through difficult landscapes. As he traveled, he saw a great deal of suffering and conflict, getting more discouraged each day. Finally, he happened upon a shop that promised him his heart's desires. The pilgrim asked for peace—within his family and the world. He asked for health, for freedom for all, and many other good things. The shopkeeper, looking very downcast, apologized to the man. "I should have explained. We don't supply the fruits here. We only supply the seeds."[3]

In transitions God provides the seeds; what we do with them is up to us. We can toss them in a drawer and forget about them. Or we can plant them in the garden and wait to see what grows next spring. God can work with anything—good and bad decisions alike—and still help us create our lives out of the choices we've made. God can even work with our resistance to change, as Moses found out. But God always works with us and takes our concerns and anxieties seriously.

Moses' experience of God at the burning bush is a prime ex-

For it was you who formed my inward parts; you knit me together in my mother's womb.

I praise you, for I am fearfully and wonderfully made. Wonderful are your works; that I know very well.

My frame was not hidden from you, when I was being made in secret, intricately woven in the depths of the earth.

Your eyes beheld my unformed substance.

—PSALM 139:13–16

ample of God's willingness to work with and even negotiate with us (Exodus 3–7). Moses wasn't at all sure about God's instruction to go back to Egypt and free the Israelites from the Egyptians, and he had a long list of arguments for God. God didn't back down from the original intent, but the Holy One gave Moses help in the form of Aaron. As biblical scholar Terrence Fretheim points out, God is willing to work, even with our fears and stubbornness. "In the face of Moses' resistance, God must resort to Plan B, calling Aaron to be Moses' voice," writes Fretheim. "Obviously, God is not delighted with this option. . . . But God goes with what is possible; using Aaron is now the best option available to God."[4]

God is willing to take Moses seriously, to adjust if need be, because God is engaged in creating the world with us, not unilaterally directing our actions. I'm not sure Fretheim is right about plan B being a less desirable option than plan A. In fact, I suspect that plan Q is just as good as plan A. God is infinitely flexible and can work with a wide variety of options. The co-creative process that God and Moses model in Exodus is one we can count on in transitions as well, for God brings to us the same invitation to co-create, as Fretheim says:

> This exchange reveals something of the nature of God's relationship with Moses. God does not adopt a take it or leave it attitude toward what God has said. God is open to disagreement, argument, even challenge on Moses' part. God is clearly the authority, but God's approach to Moses within relationship is nonauthoritarian in nature. It is more than simply divine patience; it is an openness to consider seriously what the human partner has to say. God's way into the future is thus not dictated solely by the divine word and will. God will take into account the perspective of the human party.[5]

That our opinions and needs are taken into account doesn't mean that God doesn't have hopes and desires for us and for all of creation. God is serious about encouraging each of us to play our part in making God's dreams a reality. And, as with Moses, God will continue to argue and push for the fulfillment of those dreams. The invitation to co-create with God, with plans B or Z, will come over and over until we are ready to accept it.

∿ Give Me a Sign ∿

It's one thing to understand, intellectually, that God is our partner in re-creating our lives. It's another to actually live with that reality. Most of us, myself included, would rather that God just give us a sign indicating which way we're supposed to go. Moses found himself in just such an uncomfortable spot. Like many of the Israelites and like many of us who still try to live faithfully, Moses wanted a sign that he was really supposed to do what God was requesting. God gave him a whole bunch of signs. God turned Moses' staff into a snake, made his hand leprous, and then healed it—and promised Moses at least a dozen other signs if that wasn't enough. (Remember that old saying: "Be careful what you ask for"?)

Moses certainly got the signs he needed to move forward, and there are days I envy him. I'd like signs that are obvious. The least God could do is come down and put a gold star on my forehead when I get the right answer. Or appear in my bathroom and have a chat with me like he does in the movie *Oh, God!* Anything would do. I'm not picky.

Unfortunately, the signs most of us get aren't quite so clear cut, but there are subtle signs—so-called coincidences, comments we receive, dreams, something we see—that give us a sense of knowing what path to take. That's why it's so essential to pay attention and look hopefully for ways in which God might be speaking and inviting us to move ahead.

Sometimes those signs come in the form of other people. Maybe you've seen *Joan of Arcadia*—a popular television show about a high school student who gets regular visits and instructions from God, who keeps taking different forms. One day God is a telephone repairman and another day a young mother with a baby in a stroller. Joan learns to recognize that God can take any form. And though I'm not sure that God takes the form of some people I run into, I do find that God speaks through all of us at various times, perhaps more often than we recognize.

In my own major moments of transition, I've sensed God's desires for my life in a variety of ways. When I moved across the country as a single person and found myself alone in a new place, one that I found lonely and difficult for the first year, I had to learn to sense God's desires in my loneliness and watch for invitations from colleagues and others. These people, one by one, invited me into new life in a land that didn't instantly feel like my own. In my recent travels with multiple sclerosis, God has continually invited me to slow down, speaking to me through my body, which stubbornly refuses to go at the same speed it used to manage easily. The signs we are given, when we're watching for them, are more subtle than sticks becoming serpents and hands magically becoming leprous and then cured. But they exist nonetheless.

An exercise I've recommended elsewhere[6] may help you learn to watch more attentively for God's presence in your life. In the prayer of examen, you set aside time to follow a simple discipline daily or weekly that can open you to all kinds of insights. Here's how it is done:

- Quiet yourself, breathe easily, and try to let go of whatever is on your mind for a little while.

- Once quieted, review the last twenty-four hours, or the last week if this is being done weekly. Try to remember the things you did, the people you saw, the thoughts or experiences that came to you.

- As you do this, look for ways in which God might have been present in any part of your day and think about the ways in which you believe you cooperated with God's hopes for you. Don't limit yourself to activities that seem religious or spiritual to you. God isn't only present to us in our prayer or worship times. And don't worry about wrong answers either; there aren't any wrong answers. God is far more present in our everyday activities than we recognize most of the time, and we give ourselves too little credit sometimes for the listening and responses we really make.

- Look for ways in which the Holy One might have been present, but you resisted the guidance. The point of this exercise isn't to beat yourself up about the ways in which you resisted God but to begin to notice that guidance on a regular basis and to notice where you feel yourself resisting. It isn't necessary to do anything but notice what's going on.

- Noticing is the first step toward being able to respond so you can continue along on your journey. Record what you're discovering about how you've both cooperated with and resisted God in the midst of your transition. You may see some interesting patterns develop over time. You may also discover that you're working with God more often than you think.

∿ Living Without Answers ∿

God invites all of us to be co-creators, during transitions and all the rest of our days, but it is just that—an invitation. We always have a choice about accepting the invitation. A wise psychologist once taught me that we always have choices in our life; even choosing not to choose is a choice. And sometimes the sheer discomfort of transitions—living in limbo without answers—tempts us to take the opposite route and cut God out of the creative process, taking over the Creator's role for ourselves.

The Israelites had a hard time getting the concept of co-creation. They either whined that God wasn't providing for them, or they tried to cut God out and create what they thought they wanted on their own. The golden calf is a perfect example. While Moses was up on the mountain receiving instructions from God for longer than they liked, the people grew impatient. They implored Aaron to build them a new god; they melted down their gold, built a golden calf, and began to worship it. And they did this after God had been present to them in huge displays of thunder and lightning and loud trumpet blasts on Mt. Sinai. They wanted a god who was more present, more tangible, more of their own making. And that's not so different from our own impulses when we feel the absence of God or of God's guidance and answers in the midst of transition. We want a god who will take care of whatever needs healing or deciding, a god that's visible and clear and tells us exactly how to move forward in the journey. And if that guidance isn't immediately available, we want answers—any answers—and an end to ambiguity. We want it now, not next week or next month.

Last fall a friend and I were hiking up a steep path that led to a glorious view of the brilliant fall foliage in the valley below. I'd taken that climb before and knew what to expect. I knew the view at the top of the trail was worth the panting and effort on the way up. On our way back down, we met some college students going up. Each of them carried a backpack, and they were winded, as we had been as we'd climbed up. "How far is it to the top?" asked one of the stronger-looking men.

"A ways," we told him, "but this is the most difficult part of the trail. You're making good progress." He smiled and seemed satisfied with the answer. A minute or two later, one of the young women in the group crossed paths with us and asked the same question. "Are we close to the top?"

"Well, it's a ways yet, but this is the hardest part. It'll get easier," we told her, truthfully.

"That's not what I want to hear. Tell me sweet lies," she answered with a little laugh.

"You're almost there," we lied.

In the midst of transition, living with sweet lies is sometimes easier than living without an answer. But the sweet lies and the other answers we can create for ourselves without any effort are impotent; they only stall the groping and searching we have to do while in the desert. One of the most challenging parts of transitions is learning to live without answers for a time, with not knowing what or where Canaan might be and how far away it is right now.

> *Create in me a clean heart, O God, and put a new and right spirit within me.*
>
> —PSALM 51:10

We all have a collection of sweet little lies. As I've learned to live with the fatigue that multiple sclerosis brings, I find myself, at least on occasion, thinking (or hoping) that the fatigue is temporary. It's one of my favorite sweet lies. You may find it very helpful to become conscious of those you tell yourself in the midst of the desert.

Spend some time thinking about the "sweet lies" and "golden calves" that tempt you during restless times. Find a place where you can be alone and quiet for a while. Sit comfortably; close your eyes if you wish and breathe normally. Focus on your breathing, and just try to clear your mind of the day's agendas and concerns. After you have relaxed for a few minutes, turn your attention to the sweet lies and golden calves in your life right now.

- What are the sweet little lies—the things you wish were true—that tempt you? If the lies were to assume the shape of an image or object, what would it be?
- What golden calves have you created or are you tempted to create to help you through difficult times? The Israelites imaged God as a golden calf. How would you image the god you want to create?
- Keep a record of anything that tempts you in your journal. Feel free to use words, but don't be afraid to draw images that come to you or to create collages of images or words cut from newspapers or magazines. This isn't an art project, and no one else has to see it, so put anything that you wish into your journal. Sometimes pictures, even abstract shapes or lines or colors, speak louder to us than words.

◡ Make It Easy, Lord ◡

The fact that we have God as a partner doesn't mean that being creative in the midst of transition is easy. A clergy friend of mine, who has accepted a new job that entails moving his family a couple of states away, is in the midst of saying his farewells to his congregation—an exhausting process. I called him one day to check on a few things and asked, as people do, how he was. "Fine," he responded, "unless we're telling the truth." He went on to tell

*Rise up
from the valley of suffering, O God,
with healing in Your wings.*

Heal the hurt within us.

Heal the wounds inflicted upon us.

Heal the memories that haunt us.

Heal the feelings that drag us down.

*Place within us the potential
to facilitate our own wellness.*

*Be wholly in us
who hunger for wholeness
every day of our lives.*

Amen.[7]

me how wearing it was to keep saying goodbye to folks for so many weeks. He feels the way I have felt in my own transitions: he'd very much like to get there now and make the whole process easier.

In a popular children's book, *The Velveteen Rabbit*, the velveteen rabbit (a child's toy) wants to become Real—a real live rabbit. Or rather, he wants to become Real immediately, without any pain or challenge. But that's not the way it works. Skin Horse, the elder toy in the nursery, explains:

> It doesn't happen all at once. . . . You become. It takes a long time. That's why it doesn't happen to people who break easily, or have sharp edges, or who have to be carefully kept. Generally, by the time you are Real, most of your hair has been loved off, and your eyes drop out and you get loose in the joints and very shabby. But these things don't matter at all, because once you are Real you can't be ugly, except to people who don't understand.[8]

The velveteen rabbit still wanted to be Real, but "the idea of growing shabby and losing his eyes and whiskers was rather sad. He wished he could become it without these uncomfortable things happening to him."[9]

The Israelites, too, wanted to make the transition from being slaves to being the people of God without the pain and tribulations of their journey. They complained with the frequency of a child going through the terrible twos. They wanted water. Then food. Having been given manna to eat, they now wanted meat It's not that their demands and fears weren't legitimate. Sometimes they were. Sometimes ours are as well. But it was their childish resistance to "growing shabby and uncomfortable"—to doing some of the creating themselves—that often angered God.

Maybe you heard the story in the news a while ago about dirt and children. Scientists have proven that children who are exposed to the normal bacteria, pet fur, and the like build up stronger immune systems than children who are washed all the time with antibacterial soap, whose toys and surroundings are constantly sterilized. In much the same way, successful transitions involve adjustment to the mess and disorder and dirt of change. The mess—for better or for worse—is part of the process and helps us become stronger.

That doesn't mean that God inflicts difficulty and suffering on us in order to make us strong. God doesn't make the mess. The transition does. In fact, God provides what we most need during times of transition, just as the Israelites got the food and water they needed to survive in the desert. But just as the velveteen rabbit had to endure the process of becoming Real, so must we live into the hopes and desires of God. The newly single person has to learn to love her new single life if she wants to be partnered again. The person diagnosed with a chronic illness has to learn to take the medicines, do the exercises, eat properly, rest, or whatever else it takes to live as fully as possible. We simply have to live with the messiness for as long as it takes.

God didn't take the Israelites directly to the promised land, to the place of milk and honey. The people weren't ready to enter

Canaan yet, any more than the velveteen rabbit was ready to be Real early in his time in the nursery. The same kind of messy, challenging, and confusing journeys lie ahead of all of us, and there will be days when that's overwhelming, when all we can think of is going back. But God willing—and God is willing—in time we may also come to find the messiness pleasing and generative.

To have a lovely garden in the spring, you have to be willing to get down in the dirt, pull weeds, plant bulbs, and get some dirt under your fingernails and on your knees and elbows. If you want to be Real, like the rabbit, or get to Canaan, like the Israelites, you'll have to live with some messiness for a while. Use your journal to keep track of the messiness that you find yourself dealing with in the midst of your transitions, your feelings about the messes, and how they affect you.

∿ Creating a Space for God ∿

Anthony De Mello tells a story of a very cold winter's night, when a man knocked on the door of a Buddhist temple and asked for shelter. The temple priest didn't normally provide accommodations for travelers, but the night was cold. "You can stay for tonight only," he told the traveler. "But only for the night. This isn't a hotel."

In the middle of the night, the priest heard noises coming from the temple and rushed to see what in the world the visitor could be doing. There he found the man sitting in front of a fire that he'd created, and the wooden statue of the Buddha was missing. "What have you done?" the priest cried.

The visitor apologized but said that the cold was too powerful, and he simply had to get a little warm.

"But you've burned the Buddha," the priest shouted. "How could you burn the Buddha?"

The fire was nearly out by this time, and the visitor sat quietly next to it, stirring the embers with a stick. "Answer me," said the priest. "Why are you just sitting there playing with the embers?"

"I'm looking for the bones of the Buddha," said the visitor.[10]

Messiness opens all kinds of doors for creative energies to flow through. Disorder—life tossed upside down or inside out—is an invitation to find new order, an invitation the priest in the story ignored. He could have spent the evening talking with his visitor, perhaps hearing stories or ideas that were new to him. Instead, he refused to let the man interrupt his usual routine any

All look to you to give them their food in due season;

when you give to them, they gather it up; when you open your hand, they are filled with good things.

When you hide your face, they are dismayed; when you take away their breath, they die and return to their dust.

When you send forth your spirit, they are created; and you renew the face of the ground.

—Psalm 104:27–30

more than necessary, until the visitor jogged him, rather forcefully, out of his normal patterns. Transitions and all the messiness they entail invite us (sometimes forcefully) to see the wooden statue for what it is (only a statue, a representation of the real thing, not the thing itself), break the rules, and try something different. They invite us to be creative and open and to trust that guidance will come in due time.

In Exodus, God, through Moses, invites the Israelites to help create some order in the midst of the chaos of their desert journey. The people are frustrated, discombobulated, and anxious, so God gives them detailed instructions for creating the tabernacle—a place where God will dwell.

Many biblical scholars say that just as God created the world in Genesis, so God creates some order for the Israelites in Exodus. The Israelites build the tabernacle according to God's specifications, much as God created the world in Genesis (Exodus 25–31). But this time, God and the Israelites are creating together. "This is one spot in the midst of a world of disorder," writes Terrence Fretheim of the tabernacle, "where God's creative, ordering work is completed according to the divine intention just as it was in the beginning. At this small, lonely place in the midst of the chaos of the wilderness, a new creation comes into being."[11] God has the plan, while the Israelites have the hands and minds to find the materials to build the tabernacle. Creating together with God is part of the process of leaving behind slavery and learning to become the people of God. Neither they nor God can build the tabernacle alone. And in doing this work together, they make a place for God to dwell in and among the people rather than on mountaintops. In much the same way, we must also create spaces for God to dwell with us and guide us in the midst of our transitions.

It would be lovely if God would provide clear instructions for creating a visible sign of the Divine presence in our lives, as in the building of the tabernacle, but that rarely happens. In fact, God sometimes seems to be AWOL in our difficult transitions. In one difficult time during my own life, I dreamed repeatedly of falling into black darkness for eternity. In the midst of the darkness, nothing was visible. Night after night I just continued to dream that I was falling into a completely dark and bottomless pit. But one night a small ledge, dimly lit by a small fire, appeared in the darkness, and I landed on it. That small light was my promise of God's presence. It was the space I had finally created for God, and I continue to visit that light in my imagination. It's my reminder of God's presence in the midst of what sometimes seems to be divine absence. God is always present, whether we can sense it at the moment or not. One of the tasks in the midst of transition is to keep demanding and looking for and noticing signs of God's presence along the way, to trust that God comes along with us, even when we don't understand or sense it.

The work of making space for God in transition can best be done by getting your creative juices going. Too often in life, certainly in the midst of a stressful transition, change looks hopeless or impossible. Those famous seven words—*But we've always done it this way*—are among the greatest enemies of transitions. Getting the creative juices going drives those words

For giving me desire,

An eager thirst, a burning ardent fire,

A virgin infant flame,

A love with which into the world I came,

An inward hidden heavenly love,

Which in my soul did work and move,

And ever ever me inflame,

With restless longing heavenly avarice,

That did incessantly a Paradise

Unknown suggest, and something undescribed

Discern, and bear me to it; be

Thy name for ever praised by me.

—THOMAS TRAHERNE

and thoughts away, and opens up doors we didn't know were there.

Getting your creative self in gear can take different forms for each of us. Keep a running list of ideas for creative ventures in your transitions journal.

What kinds of things seem to be drawing you? Art classes? Writing? Gardening? Hiking? Dancing? Community theater? Don't worry about the practicality of the idea at this point; just write down anything that seems to be speaking to you.

Look at your list periodically, and make a point of acting on one or more of those ideas. Maybe it means trying out an art project of some kind—something you haven't done before. Or maybe it means joining an exercise class and experimenting with new physical sensations and images. There's cooking, and there are classes and social opportunities of all sorts, as well as volunteer programs.

Notice your fears about trying something new, if you feel them, but don't let them stop you from trying something creative and fun.

The form of creativity you choose doesn't matter; it only matters that you use your creative energies to try new things. You don't have to be good at whatever you try. That's not the point. Remember what Isaiah said: "I am about to do a new thing." We're hardly ever good at new things right off the bat. In her book for preachers, professor Linda Clader recommends that they learn to be comfortable being amateurs and stop trying to be experts all the time. Being an amateur leaves room for the Holy Spirit to come in and do creative things with our hearts and souls.[12] Her advice holds not only for preachers but for all of us. In the midst of transition, stop worrying about being competent. Moses took lots of missteps and made mistakes all the time; God didn't abandon him, and the people still got to Canaan. Let transition be a time of openness to the new, of being an amateur and not worrying about it. Transitions are about creating something new, in concert with God. So try something new. Try lots of new things. Like Moses, you'll probably be surprised by what develops.

What develops for most of us, at least for a while, of course, is more messiness. And viewing that messiness as an invitation to create something new can grow tiresome. If God is about to create something new, there are days when I'd just as soon God get on with it already. Sometimes we want answers so badly that we accept the first one that comes along or the first one we can create. It seems easier and better than cultivating the patience and attention required to co-create with God. We build our own golden calf and hope it will give us what we want.

The problem is that the golden calves we create for ourselves are empty and impotent. When we try to make God over in our own image, instead of letting God co-create us, we get something that may be satisfying for the moment but has no creative power. In times of crisis, it can do nothing to help. It can't help us grow; it teaches nothing about love. The god we can create on our own is just a sterile object or set of beliefs, and relationship with it is static and limiting. What, after all, could the Israelites' golden calf do for them? Was it going to guide them to Canaan or give them laws to live by or food and water when they were hungry?

Though God won't abandon us if we don't accept the invitation to share in the creation of our future—God's patience *is* infinite—there are consequences for declining the invitation. The main one is that we won't grow and thrive; we won't become what Roman Catholic priest and writer Henri Nouwen speaks of as fruitful, or fecund.

> The great mystery of fecundity is that it becomes visible where we have given up our attempts to control life and take the risk to let life reveal its own inner movements. Whenever we trust and surrender ourselves to the God of love, fruits will grow. Fruits can only come forth from the ground of intimate love. They are not made, nor are they the result

of specific human actions that can be repeated. Neither pre-dictable nor definable, fruits are gifts to be received.[13]

We can only receive those gifts if we have accepted the invi-tation to co-create with God. Only then can we move forward to the promised land that God has set aside for us.

I want to add an important caveat to this, however. There are times in the desert journey that we're just plain too tired to be cre-ative. A friend of mine recently underwent an operation, and the recovery is taking longer than she wishes it would. She's got a book she wants to write and lots of other things to do. And she's too exhausted to do any of it. There are times for creativity and co-cre-ating with God in the midst of transition, and there are times to rest, something I'll talk more about in a future chapter. When it's time to rest, do that. There will be days for creativity later on.

> *O God of peace, who has taught us that in returning and rest we shall be saved, in quietness and in confidence shall be our strength: By the might of your Spirit lift us, we pray, to your presence, where we may be still and know that you are God; through Jesus Christ our Lord. Amen.*
>
> —THE BOOK OF COMMON PRAYER 1979, ADAPTED

Transitions can bring out the worst in any of us, of course, just as the desert sojourn did for the Israelites. Even Moses had his off moments. Transitions are always trying.

Self-help books promise guidance through every difficulty known to humankind, offering step-by-step instructions so that moving forward will be painless. They lure us with the promise of expert guidance so we won't make any mistakes, and we'll get to our goal with no fuss or muss. Beneath their methods lies the assumption that we can become our own creators. There's nothing wrong with good advice, especially from those who've already been down a road you're just starting on. But it's an illusion to believe that anything can make the road smooth, without potholes, and that you can make the journey without getting shabby and uncomfortable. Transitions invite us to make a space for God on the journey, to let go of the reins and be creative in new ways. They invite us to take one step after another, praying all the while for traveling mercies, in confidence that God, who loves us, will be with us each step of the way.

> *O Christ, our Morning Star, Splendor of Light Eternal, shining with the glory of the rainbow, come and waken us from the grayness of our apathy and renew in us your gift of hope.*
>
> —THE VENERABLE BEDE

O Lord, when Thou didst call me, didst Thou know
My heart disheartened through and through,
Still hankering after Egypt full in view
Where cucumbers and melons grow?
       —"Yea, I knew."—
But, Lord, when Thou didst choose me, didst Thou know
How marred I was and withered too,
Nor rose for sweetness nor for virtue rue,
Timid and rash, hasty and slow?
       —"Yea, I knew."—
My Lord, when Thou didst love me, didst Thou know
How weak my efforts were, how few,
Tepid to love and impotent to do,
Envious to reap while slack to sow?

—*"Yea, I knew."*—
Good Lord, Who knowest what I cannot know
And dare not know, my false, my true,
My new, my old; Good Lord, arise and do
Where cucumbers anknown me so.
—*"Yea, I knew."*—
—Christina Rossetti[14]

CHAPTER III

Help!

*O merciful God, who has taught us in your holy Word
that you do not willingly afflict or grieve us:
Look with pity upon the sorrows of your servants
for whom our prayers are offered. Remember us,
O Lord, in mercy, nourish our soul with patience,
comfort us with a sense of your goodness, lift up your
countenance upon us, and give us peace; through
Jesus Christ our Lord. Amen.*[1]
—BOOK OF COMMON PRAYER 1979

I sat in church near the altar on a Thursday evening in April, waiting for it all to begin," writes journalist Nora Gallagher, at the beginning of her memoir *Practicing Resurrection*. She goes on to describe the people who enter the church for the service, ending with the priest who settles in to begin an evening prayer service. Just as the service begins, a stranger enters the church. The stranger "with dirty clothes and a stubbled chin walked unevenly into the church and sat down in a shadowed pew," writes Gallagher.

> He had "homeless" written all over him. Probably drunk. Mark [the priest] motioned for him to come up to the altar area. He staggered slightly as he climbed the steps. When we stood for the Gospel reading, he reached for Mark's hand and held onto it, his finger's knotted in Mark's like lovers, for the rest of the service.[2]

That simple and moving story illustrates the importance and power of asking for, and accepting, help in the midst of transitions. The man, probably drunk and homeless, wandered into a community that offered him support and acceptance. . . . The help they gave was simple rather than dramatic. The homeless man probably needed more help than this in the long run, but for the moment, he got the acceptance he needed. The welcoming congregation and the priest clasping the man's hand throughout the service was enough for the moment. At the end of the service, his hand still entwined with the priest's, he raised his hand and blessed the small congregation gathered at the altar.

We too must find ways to look for, ask for, and gratefully accept the help, support, and encouragement of others in the midst of traveling through the desert lands of our lives. But relying on the "kindness of strangers," as Blanche DuBois says in the famous line from the play "A Streetcar Named Desire," or even on the kindness of friends, family, and loved ones can be difficult. Think about all the responses the homeless man might have received to his presence at the evening prayer service. The congregation could have been repulsed by his appearance. They could have let him sit in the back of the church rather than invite him into their intimate circle around the altar. They might even have decided to lock the front door in the future to prevent other homeless people from wandering in. The priest could have refused the man's hand or held it for a moment and then let go. The unnamed homeless man made himself vulnerable when he asked for help, and the congregation made itself vulnerable in response, offering what help they could. As a result of the mutual vulnerability, everyone present was enriched and blessed. But just the opposite could have happened; vulnerable and hurting people are disappointed all the time. Most of us have a story or two to tell of being turned away in a moment of need.

> *Out of the depths have I called to you, O Lord;*
>
> *Lord, hear my voice;*
>
> *let your ears consider well the voice of my supplication.*
>
> —PSALM 130:1 (THE BOOK OF COMMON PRAYER 1979)

We can identify with the Israelites and their struggle with being vulnerable. Over and over they worried that God would abandon them to a fate worse than being slaves in Egypt. They seemed to prefer what they knew—a life in slavery—to the place Moses and God were leading them. They struggled with learning to ask for help. More often than not, they complained when they felt anxious instead of being forthright with Moses or God; they accused God and Moses of making their lives more difficult. As the Israelites fled Egypt, with the Egyptians pursuing them from behind and a sea of water in front of them, they panicked. "Was it because there were no graves in Egypt that you have taken us away to die in the wilderness?" they cried to Moses (Exodus 14:11). "Do not be afraid," responds Moses. "Stand firm, and see the deliverance that the LORD will accomplish for you today; for the Egyptians whom you see today you shall never see again. The LORD will fight for you, and you have only to keep still" (Exodus 14:13–14). Those were good and prophetic words, but I suspect I would have felt the same annoyance and fear the Israelites did at being told to be still when surrounded by danger on all sides.

Was it because there were no graves in Egypt that you have taken us away to die in the wilderness?

—EXODUS 14:11

Standing still would have been the last thing I'd have wanted to do. Trusting that God will provide the help needed, in one form or another, is just plain difficult.

God saved the Israelites by parting the sea and letting them through safely, but three days later, with no water in sight, the people grew anxious again. Whenever they felt vulnerable, their trust in God's (and Moses') ability to help disappeared quickly, as is so often the case. God, ever patient, showed Moses how to sweeten the bitter waters of Mar'ah so the people could drink. Still the people feared their vulnerability and complained again when they had no food. And who could blame them? God provided manna and quail for the people to eat and renewed the availability of the manna six days a week. But the Israelites continued to struggle with their vulnerability. And rather than admit their vulnerability to God and ask for God's help, they continued to rail against God and Moses.

Sometimes reading this story, it seems as though the Israelites were a spoiled and shallow people, but at other times it's not hard to relate to their fears and to their reactions. Being angry or blaming others for the challenges in transitions and the fears that arise is easier than asking for help. Admitting helplessness in times of transition (much less other times in our lives) leaves us vulnerable, especially when we don't know whether help will be given or what form that help may take. There are so many reasons to resist asking for the very help we need.

∾ Blaming the Victim ∾

Sometimes we resist making our needs known to others because we're afraid we'll be blamed for whatever difficulty we find ourselves in. Mary Earle, in her book *Broken Body, Healing Spirit*, writes about others' responses to her pancreatitis while she lay ill.

> In the hospital following my first attack, friends, parishioners, and fellow clergy came to see me, and rare was the visitor who didn't come with an interpretation—almost all unhelpful—of my illness. . . . Since my pancreas was the affected organ, I was told that I didn't have enough sweetness in my life, presumably because the pancreas, in its creation of insulin, regulates blood sugar levels.[3]

So often it's easier for people to find explanations for whatever ill confronts someone than to deal with the reality that things happen over which we have no control. A young baby dies suddenly and without explanation, and someone tells the parents that God wanted their angel in Heaven. Or someone who is living with enormous and unrelenting pain is reminded that, "God never gives us more than we can bear." The explanations are meant to be comforting, but most of the time they end up leaving the suffering person suffering more.

Far too often, as was true for Mary Earle in her time of illness and need, the fear of being blamed turns out to be legitimate. In an episode of a popular television show, "The West Wing," one character, Leo, tells his friend Jed that his wife has asked him for a divorce. Jed accuses Leo of ignoring his wife (which is true) and demands that he fix the situation. Leo, who has withheld news of his divorce from Jed for several weeks because he feared that his friend would blame him, sees his worst fears realized. Only later does Jed apologize to Leo, who is feeling bad enough that his job has destroyed his marriage. Having this pointed out to him and being blamed, forcefully, for his predicament wasn't helpful. Jed finally realizes this and comes not only to apologize but to offer any help Leo might need. Right relationship is restored between the two friends.

Abide with me; fast falls the eventide;

The darkness deepens; Lord with me abide;

When other helpers fail, and comforts flee,

Help of the helpless, O abide with me.

I need thy presence every passing hour;

What but thy grace can foil the tempter's power?

Who like thyself my guide and stay can be?

Through cloud and sunshine, Lord, abide with me.

—HENRY FRANCIS LYTE

The stories of Mary Earle and Jed and Leo illustrate the concern that asking for help will lead to being blamed for a difficult transition. A fair chunk of Christian theology and spirituality over the centuries was based on exactly this notion. Whether or not the transition is the result of something over which we have control (as Leo might have) isn't the issue. Some transitions do come about as a result of our own errors, but once we're in the midst of the transition, it doesn't really matter whether we caused it or not. No matter what spurred the desert journey, the simple fact of our being in transition makes other people uncomfortable.

Some people fear having to make a similar journey in their own lives. It's as if being around someone who is coping with the difficult emotions around divorce, the loss of a loved one, or loneliness in a new community is going to be contagious somehow. We don't like being reminded that these kinds of transitions are possible in our own lives, so we push away those in pain or discomfort. Another story from the Desert Fathers speaks of a young monk who is scolded by an older one for his admission that he has lustful thoughts from time to time. The older monk, outraged, tells the younger one that he shouldn't even be a monk. A more mature monk helps the younger one eventually, but I can't help but wonder if the scolding older monk responded to the younger one so forcefully because he had lustful thoughts of his own from time to time and didn't like being reminded of his own shortcomings.

Transitions—discomfort in the desert—sometimes get interpreted as failure. If things were right with our lives, if God was happy with how we were living, all would be well, or so the argument goes. Too often we believe, as Job's unhelpful friends did, that any difficult time in our own lives or the lives of others must be the result of failure, and the transitional time is God's punishment. "Perhaps we still have a basically superstitious tendency to associate failure with dishonesty and guilt—failure being interpreted as 'punishment,'" writes Trappist monk Thomas Merton.

> Even if a man starts out with good intentions, if he fails we tend to think he was somehow "at fault." If he was not guilty, he was at least "wrong." And "being wrong" is something we have not yet learned to face with equanimity and understanding. We either condemn it with god-like disdain or forgive it with god-like condescension. We do not manage to accept it with human compassion, humility, and identification.[4]

The homeless man in Nora Gallagher's story could easily have gotten such a response. How often do we simply walk by homeless people on the streets, not even acknowledging their presence, because they make us uncomfortable and because we fear our own homelessness? How often do we ignore the man who has been downsized from his job . . . or the woman living with breast cancer . . . or the teenager struggling with disability? . . . Blaming people for the difficulties of the desert life is easier than facing the fact that desert times happen to all people sooner or later.

> *Arise, O sun of righteousness, upon us, with healing in thy wings; make us children of the light and of the day. Show us the way in which we should walk, for unto thee, O Lord, do we lift up our souls. Dispel all mists of ignorance which cloud our understandings. Let no false suggestion either withdraw our hearts from the love of thy truth, or from the practice of it in all the actions of our lives; for the sake of Jesus Christ our Lord.*
>
> —THOMAS SHERLOCK

At other times friends simply don't know what to say to someone in a transition. Their own inability to fix things, to make everything right again, leaves them feeling helpless, and their distress turns into discomfort. Bill Williams, who died in 1998 of cystic fibrosis, wrote in his book, *Naked Before God,* about how uncomfortable his disease was for others. Speaking of the Christian response to illness (though Bill's words apply equally to other uncomfortable transitions), he writes:

> Prayer is an obvious response to illness; and if the illness is a broken leg or fever, it should not feel condemning. But if the sickness is part of your very formation, it can also feel like a rejection of *who you are,* who you have to be. To hurry

up and pray for a Down's syndrome child may be an expression of your own revulsion; it may be an indication of your anxiety, not his need.[5]

What Bill Williams found most helpful in his life was the presence of people who were not anxious about his condition, people with whom he could just be himself and from whom he didn't need to hide his discomfort. The homeless man, in the story at the beginning of the chapter, found the same accepting, compassionate presence in the congregation. Even Moses needed the help of someone who knew more than he did—someone who wasn't anxious about the path ahead and who could help guide him. In Numbers, as the people set out from Sinai, Moses asked Hobab—a member of the Midianites, a nomadic people—to accompany the Israelites on their journey. "We are setting out for the place of which the LORD said, 'I will give it to you,'" Moses says to Hobab. "Come with us, and we will treat you well; for the LORD has promised good to Israel." Hobab wanted to return to his own people, but Moses asked again. "Do not leave us, for you know where we should camp in the wilderness, and you will serve as eyes for us. Moreover, if you go with us, whatever good the LORD does for us, the same we will do for you" (Numbers 10:29–32).

 We have but faith; we cannot know;

For knowledge is of things we see;

And yet we trust it comes from Thee,

A beam in darkness: let it grow.

—ALFRED LORD TENNYSON

While wandering through desert times, it is good to seek out the people who can accompany us without anxiety, without blaming us. Just as God's assistance for the Israelites often came through Moses, God's care for each of us usually comes through caring people who resist blame and who don't become anxious in the presence of difficulty. Like Job, Bill Williams, or Mary Earle, we need to refuse to accept the blame placed on us by people who are uncomfortable with transitions and look for those who have the gift of being God's hands and feet and heart.

Like the Israelites, we are invited to rely on God's guidance and wisdom through connections with others, particularly those who have already taken similar journeys and who can provide at least a partial roadmap of the way forward. That's why Alcoholics Anonymous and other support groups have been so helpful and spiritually nourishing to people who are trying to transition from one way of life to another. It's the combination of seeking help from what AA calls a Higher Power—and I call God—combined with the help of those who have already taken the journey that is so powerful.

Read the story of the Israelites' journey in the second year and Moses' invitation to Hobab in Numbers 10:11–33. Spend some time journaling about this story, using either the following questions or ones that speak to you.

- As you read the story of Moses and Hobab, which character is more like you? Imagine yourself as a character in the story itself, and notice how you feel. Write down any emotions you sense.
- Think of a time when you looked to someone for help and didn't receive it. What feelings do you still have about that situation? Do they affect your current willingness to ask for help?
- Who are the people in your own life who are calm, compassionate, and accepting? Are some of those people good ones to ask for any assistance you need? What, if anything, prevents you from asking them for help?

When our own hands, feet, eyes, hearts, or minds aren't working at full throttle, God provides others who can help us walk, see, and think. God provides those who can nourish our souls with patience and clear thinking, those who can comfort us and hold our hands when needed. They know where to camp in the wilderness. Thanks be to God.

∿ Control and Incompetence ∿

In another story Anthony De Mello collected, Mullah Nasruddin's house was on fire. Nasruddin, unable to escape through a window or door, ran up to the roof for safety. His friends gathered on the street below and held the four corners of a large blanket and begged him to jump.

> "Oh no, I won't," says the Mullah, "I know you fellows. If I jump, you'll pull the blanket away just to make a fool of me!" His friends assured him that they only wanted to save the Mullah's life. "No," said Nasruddin. "I don't trust any of you. Lay that blanket on the ground and I'll jump."[6]

Does the story sound familiar to you? Have you—as I have—ever resisted seeking or accepting help because you're afraid to look foolish, or worse, incompetent—to give up control? At base there is something within most of us that keeps believing that we ought to be able to solve our own problems—all of them, all of the time. Children are supposed to need help; adults are not. But thinking that way means trying to *be* God instead of working in collaboration with God.

In his classic book on making transitions, William Bridges tells the story of a woman who had a difficult time adjusting to the changes required by the birth of her first child. Though this woman loved her baby, she wasn't prepared for the massive demands the child made on her schedule and her marriage. She was sure that everyone else navigated this kind of difficulty without any problems, that she alone was incompetent at mastering motherhood. She'd bought into a Norman Rockwell sort of picture of the perfect, beaming, and happy parents with their newborn infant. Bridges points out her relief at discovering that others found the transition to parenthood a difficult one, too. For this woman, "the confusion and embarrassment over not being able to manage an ordinary life experience smoothly—something [she] imagined that others managed easily"[7]—kept her from moving forward in her desert journey. Only by asking for help, by discovering that others shared her experience, could she give up trying to fix everything herself.

Moses had to learn the same kind of lesson in Exodus. Shortly after escaping from Egypt and only a little way into the desert journey, Moses was trying to do everything himself without help from anyone (Exodus 18:13–27). In this part of the story, Jethro has to come to Moses and recommended that he let others help. Moses made the classic mistake that new leaders and managers make: they fail to delegate because they're afraid to give up the controls. He didn't trust anyone else to provide guidance or assistance, just like the man who wouldn't jump from the burning roof into his friends' waiting blanket. Maybe he feared that others would think he wasn't competent to lead the Israelites. After all, leaders and managers are supposed to know everything, right? Taking charge of every little detail is particularly tempting during times of transition, when it feels impossible or difficult to control our environment and circumstances. The truth is that we never have as much control as we think we do; transitions just have a way of reminding us of that fact.

I rediscovered this all-too-human tendency for myself in the midst of writing this book. I moved to a new home part way through the writing and very sensibly took a week off from work to get moved and settled. You've probably heard the old saying: "If you want to make God laugh, tell him your plans." Not only was I going to move, get unpacked by the end of the week, and prepare my old house for sale, but all of that would be done in the first half of my week off from work. During the last few days, I planned to work on my writing, prepare for a workshop I was leading the following week, and organize a class I had to teach in two weeks. It all started out okay; in four days, I had moved and unpacked about 80 percent of the house. I was utterly exhausted, totally unable to enjoy what was being created in my new space, but still sticking to my original plan. Neighbors kindly came by and offered me food and help, which I graciously refused. ("Everything's going great! Thanks, but I think I've got everything I need.")

> *Turn, O Lord, and deliver me;*
>
> *save me for your mercy's sake.*
>
> *For in death no one remembers you;*
>
> *and who will give you thanks from the grave?*
>
> —PSALM 6:4–5 (THE BOOK OF COMMON PRAYER 1979)

In the midst of my prayer time one day, I realized that I was trying to control the move, to get everything settled immediately so that my own desert time would be truncated. After laughing at myself (and I suspect God chuckled as well), I realized that I needed to slow down, that the world wouldn't end if everything wasn't in its assigned place before I returned to work. The pictures could lean against a wall for a while, and organizing the basement could wait, too. Like Moses, I finally let go of the reins. The unpacking could happen little by little, as the new space and I grew to know each other.

Perhaps we forget that asking others for help is a gift not only to ourselves but to others as well. When we stop trying to be

God and let the Creator of it all be God, when we let God's creatures help us (and when we help others, for that matter), we participate in co-creating a world closer to what God continually
hopes for. God could have done everything there was to do in
Genesis, but instead the Holy One enlisted Adam's help in nam-
ing the animals. When Moses stopped trying to do everything
himself, at the expense of the people who were forced to wait days
to see him, and selected men to help him settle the people's con-
flicts and answer their questions, I suspect the men he appointed
were grateful for the opportunity to grow, to learn, to help. The
Israelites were certainly grateful to have their cases heard more
expeditiously. Everyone won. In the midst of the desert, sometimes
we too have to let go of our need to control everything, to know
and do everything, even when we suspect that others unreasonably
expect unlimited competence and control. We are in unknown
territory, trying to find our way to a place we've never seen, which
isn't even on the map. That's exhausting, and just the process of
continuing to walk the walk is enough to try to manage. We need
help with even the most basic functions of life sometimes, particularly in desert seasons.

*Read Exodus 18:13–27, the story of Jethro and Moses. Spend some
time journaling about the story using the following suggestions or ones
that speak more clearly to you.*

- As you consider the story of Moses and Jethro, are you
  more like a Moses or a Jethro? Imagine yourself as a character in the story, and notice the feelings you have as the
  story proceeds. Make some notes about those feelings in
  your journal.
- Spend some time thinking about what you're hanging
  onto, as Moses did, that you could let go of, either temporarily or permanently. Make a list of the activities or

responsibilities that someone else could take care of or help with. Try to be really honest with yourself.

- What arrangements can you make to off-load those tasks or responsibilities for the time being? Record your thoughts on this, and make a commitment to following through on one or more of your ideas.

∿ I Am Not Worthy ∿

Edward Hays, a Catholic priest and wonderful story teller, often writes stories or parables that convict me. I think he knows human foibles much too well. In one of them—a story about a glove—Hays highlights one of the other roadblocks faced in the desert: that sense that we're not worthy of God's attention. "O Lord, I am not worthy that you should come to me, yet say the word and I shall be healed," said the glove, in Hays's modern parable. The poor glove thought itself so worthless that it was filled with self-pity rather than a hand, and it spent its days begging God to heal it.

> "All right, all right," moaned a weary God, "I will say the word—and, kid, the word is *Relax!*"
>
> "Relax?" asked the startled glove as it wiped away a tear. "What do you mean, relax?"
>
> "Relax, let go of yourself. Forget yourself and your precious image of being a wretch, a sinful kid," answered God. "As long as you are stuffed—full of grief over your failings and your unworthiness—there's no room for me, or anyone, to come to you. So, kid, if you want to be healed, relax!"[8]

In transitions, particularly ones for which we feel some level of responsibility, it's easy to think ourselves unworthy of forgiveness or help. Perhaps a childhood image of God as wrathful father, a figure who found our bad behavior absolutely intolerable, gets in the way. Maybe we confused a parent who wasn't particularly loving or nurturing with God. Some people struggle with having been raised in a religious environment that focused more on the law than on the love of God. These can all lead to distorted images of God. None of them describes the God who responded to the Israelites' cries for liberation or the God who then traveled in the desert with them on their journey to Canaan.

Hearken to my voice, O LORD, when I call;

have mercy on me and answer me.

You speak in my heart and say, "Seek my face."

Your face, LORD, will I seek.

Hide not your face from me,

nor turn away your servant in displeasure.

You have been my helper;

cast me not away;

do not forsake me, O God of my salvation.

—PSALM 27:10–13
(THE BOOK OF COMMON PRAYER 1979)

If anyone was undeserving of God's help, it was the Israelites. Even after the miracle of their escape from Egypt, they mistrusted God nearly every step of the way. They broke God's law more often than a two-year-old throws a tantrum. Their early complaints were about things they really needed— food and water—but after a time of wandering in the desert, even with an ample supply of food and water, the people complained just because they were tired, cranky, and sick of the journey. Sometimes they complained for no apparent reason at all. And yes, that made God and Moses mad. Moses had to intercede for the people repeatedly. And sometimes Moses got so angry with the people that God's wrath looked minor. But through it all, Moses kept reminding God that they had a covenant and that God promised these people a land of milk and honey. And God honored that promise. The only people who didn't get to go into the land (aside from Moses, who was denied entrance for an unspecified violation of God's desires, described in Numbers 20) were the people who turned down entrance to Canaan when it was offered to them.

It is hard for me to imagine that anyone reading this book has been a more miserable sinner than the Israelites were in the desert. But it can be easy and comforting, while wandering in the desert, to hang on to guilt and refuse to forgive ourselves for what we've done wrong. Doing that is a subtle way of becoming the Creator again, as New Testament scholar Bill Countryman explains in his book on forgiveness:

> When I forgive myself, I'm letting go of a certain kind of useless guilt—not the simple awareness of responsibility (that's precisely what I'm accepting and acknowledging), but a self-regarding and sometimes self-dramatizing guilt that leads nowhere in particular. While I hang on to this guilt, I am subtly presenting myself as having done something so terrible that not even God can forgive it. Although this behavior has all the external appearance of humility, it's really a clever and externally pious way of making myself the center of the universe—the only person in all creation who is beyond the reach of God![9]

This sense that we have done something that God can't forgive can prevent us from truly asking for and accepting help. Someone may plead day in and day out for God to guide or heal her, but if she is closed off from God and filled with self-pity—or perhaps the arrogance—of being a great sinner or a failure or lacking in some other way, she leaves no room for God. There was nothing that the Israelites could do to shake God, except to reject him and the gifts and assistance of God outright, and that is true for us as well.

◡ Fearful Answers ◡

"I don't want to be a missionary in Africa." That's what one of the students in a class of mine said. She thought it might be better to avoid discerning God's desires for her or asking for any help,

> ✠ *Give ear to my words, O Lord;*
>
> *consider my meditation.*
>
> *Hearken to my cry for help, my King and my God,*
>
> *for I make my prayer to you.*
>
> —PSALM 5:1–2 (THE BOOK OF COMMON PRAYER 1979)

because she wasn't really sure she'd like the answers she'd get. She was a smart woman—smart enough to know that God's help may be what she needed but was not always the kind of help she'd actually like to receive.

Her comment reminded me of a story from Theodore of Pherme, another Desert Father. He tells about a monk who had lived a solitary life in his cell but who couldn't find the sense of peacefulness that he'd expected from his solitude. He asked

Theodore for advice, and Theodore told him to go live with others, under the obedience of a superior. Some time later, the man returned to Theodore complaining that he had not found peace in community either. The story continues:

> The old man said to him, "If you are not at peace either alone or with others, why have you become a monk? Is it not to suffer trials? Tell me how many years you have worn the habit?" He replied, "For eight years." Then the old man said to him, "I have worn the habit seventy years and on no day have I found peace. Do you expect to obtain peace in eight years?" At these words the brother went away strengthened.[10]

I'm glad the brother went away strengthened; I'm not sure I would have. I think I might have been a bit more like the classic character Eeyore, in the tales of Winnie the Pooh. Eeyore, the donkey, goes around with a look of resignation on his face and responds to questions or requests with a sigh. "Oh, okay . . ." or "Oh, I'm fine . . . ," he says with a sigh and a sad look in his eyes, his head hung low, ears dragging along on the ground behind him. I love Eeyore; he makes me laugh. But Eeyore didn't want to be

 Father, I am seeking: I am hesitant and uncertain, but will you, O God, watch over each step of mine and guide me.

—ST. AUGUSTINE

challenged. He wasn't interested in difficult journeys or in expending energy or being enthusiastic. Best to just resign yourself to the world, Eeyore seems to say, and not ask any of the hard questions. You might have to do something with the answers.

It's reasonable and natural to fear change, even change for what may be the better. "The devil you know," as the old saying goes, "is better than the devil that you don't know." But that fear of change or fear of where the answers to our questions may lead is exactly what prevented some of the Israelites from entering Canaan the land promised to them. (After all, it was the Israelites' cry to God for help that set the whole Exodus story in motion in the first place.) It's as if God gave them a wrapped present, and they didn't even bother to unwrap it and see what was inside. Like the student in my class, they didn't want to "go to Africa," because they feared what they didn't know, and "Africa"—which can be a different place for everyone—may well be full of incredible challenges. There's good reason to be fearful; we may indeed get sent to Africa. But as scripture tells us repeatedly, there's reason to be hopeful as well, and Africa may end up being full of wonderful new vistas.

Spend some time making notes about whatever prevents you from moving ahead, using these questions or others that speak to you:

- What frightens you about moving forward? What places do you absolutely not want to visit?
- Why do you think this is so?
- Can you imagine any "wonderful new vistas" that might be ahead of you if you do move forward? What might they be?

∿ Answer Me When I Call, O Lord ∿

There are a variety of places to find help in the desert of transitions. Friends, family, and spiritual community can all be helpful. Even the solitary Desert Fathers and Mothers lived within range of each other and gathered on Sabbath and Holy Days to worship together. Like them, we need the ongoing and regular support of community. Sometimes, however, the most helpful people can be those outside the usual support systems. Especially when we are in transition, the help of people who have no vested interest in our decisions can be very useful. Well-meaning friends and family may encourage us, usually unconsciously, to stay within systems or situations that may not work for us anymore—systems that have little to do with what God is calling out of us—because change may send others into transition as well.

O God, our Help in ages past,

Our Hope for years to come,

Our shelter from the stormy blast,

And our eternal Home!

—ISAAC WATTS

As you consider the people or organizations that may be helpful to you in finding the way through the desert, consider the people or groups who know you well and have been helpful to you in the past. But look beyond those options as well. Support groups modeled on Alcoholic Anonymous, church, or other support groups, particularly those for people going through the same kind of transition you're going through, can be invaluable places to find support or wisdom. Many churches, as well as other institutions, provide these kinds of support groups.

Because the desert journey is a creative one, where God calls us into newness and new options, you might also consider seeing a spiritual director, even if you've never done that before. Spiritual directors differ from psychologists or psychiatrists by helping you focus on how God is moving in your life right now. They're not trying to solve problems in the same way that a psychologist or psychiatrist might be, though they may help you notice how God is leading you toward newness in your life that brings about solutions. Spiritual directors will listen to your exploration of the desert terrain you find yourself in and help you notice the landscape, both the physical landscape around you and the landscape of your own soul. A good spiritual director can help you discover that God is guiding you and where that guidance might be leading. She or he can also provide you with valuable companionship on the journey—that calm and compassionate presence that is so necessary when the terrain is unknown and frightening.[11]

And don't forget about help you might get from your healthcare practitioner. Though he may not think of himself as God's hands and feet, he may still fill that role in your transitional time. As I was trying to adjust to the medicines given to MS patients, I struggled with enormous fatigue and, finally, depression. I'd been warned that this was a common side effect of the medicines, and when I realized that I wasn't sleeping well, that I didn't have the energy to even get out of bed in the morning, much less drag myself through the workdays, I went to see my neurologist. He is a kind man and was sympathetic. He also suggested that I take an antidepressant for a while, until my body adjusted to the medicines I needed for the MS. Taking the antidepressant for a short period made a huge difference in how I felt and how I managed what needed to be done each day. My neurologist may not think of himself as God's gift to me, but he has been just that, many times.

Be thou a light unto mine eyes, music to mine ears, sweetness to my taste, and a full contentment to my heart. Be thou my sunshine in the day, my food at the table, my repose in the night, my clothing in nakedness, and my succour in all necessities.

—JOHN COSIN

It's hard to know what form help may take along the desert path. Some of it we can seek out—the support groups, medical community, spiritual directors, or clergy. Some of it comes in the form of simple kindnesses, like neighbors bringing dinners to put in the freezer so we don't have to cook, or a friend giving a ride to a doctor's appointment, or someone going grocery shopping for us or taking the kids out for the day so we can rest. Still other forms of help come from completely unexpected places, like the kindness of strangers. Accept all of it. Recognize it as the gift of God for one of God's beloved—you. And if you can't accept it on that basis, accept it as a gift that you are giving to someone else who wants to help. The time will certainly come when you can return that gift to the giver or pass the gift forward to someone else who needs it.

CHAPTER IV

Eat, Sleep, Bend, and Stretch

*O God of peace, who has taught us that in returning
and rest we shall be saved, in quietness and in
confidence shall be our strength: By the might of your
Spirit lift us, we pray, to your presence, where we may
be still and know that you are God;
through Jesus Christ our Lord. Amen.*
—THE BOOK OF COMMON PRAYER 1979

It was a ritual. Blanche, Dorothy, Rose, and Sylvia—four women in the "Golden Girls" sitcom from many years ago—in the midst of any transition or crisis gathered around the kitchen table late at night. Out came the cheesecake from the freezer, and over cheesecake the women explored whatever problem was at hand.

The idea of comfort food—something that temporarily fills the emptiness inside us—is one most of us know well. Think of all the movies that feature a woman, usually one who has lost her job or her man, who sits alone in her sweats, weeping, listening to old songs on the stereo, and eating a pint of ice cream. Ice cream and cheesecake probably aren't the healthiest choices possible in taking care of ourselves—our physical selves—in the times of transition, but they both point to the instinct and the need to pay attention to the body's needs in desert times.

Lord, sanctify us wholly, that our whole spirit, soul, and body may become thy temple.

—THOMAS KEN

It can be easy to ignore physical needs during transitions. We're not hungry, so we don't eat. We're too tired to exercise. Or we keep the miseries of transition at bay by working 24/7. But the restlessness we feel is as physical as it is spiritual or emotional. Ignoring the body's needs only prolongs the desert journey. In the midst of the desert, God invites us to take care of our physical selves. The Israelites came up against these needs almost instantly in their journey, and God responded, giving them what they needed or suggesting ways in which the people could provide for themselves. God tended to the people's needs for food and water and rest, and encouraged them to care for themselves as well. If we want to make our way through the desert, we must join God in caring, not just for our souls but for our bodies. They are inseparable.

Christian history is full of the opposite theology and spirituality, however. Back as far as the third and fourth centuries, the Desert Fathers and Mothers taught that stifling physical needs (sleeping and eating little and other bodily deprivations) led one closer to God. Throughout much of Christian history, bodily needs and sexuality were seen as barriers to the soul's progress toward God. In recent decades, however, Christians have been re-reading scripture and finding

> *O God, you are my God, I seek you, my soul thirsts for you; my flesh faints for you, as in a dry and weary land · where there is no water.*
>
> —PSALM 63:1

within it God's delight in our physicality. The stories of Exodus and Numbers, where God tends regularly to the physical needs of the Israelites, have been part of the rediscovery of the importance of the body in Christian life and spirituality.

∾ Finding the Rhythm ∾

My family converted to Reformed Judaism when I was a teenager. We'd been Unitarian and Presbyterian, and this was the next stage of my mother's religious journey. We were Jewish for several years, and some important aspects of my own spirituality were formed during those years; one was learning the importance of the rhythm of work and Sabbath rest. In the Jewish tradition, work ceases at sundown on Friday. The Shabbat, or Sabbath, dinner, with

Six days you shall work, but on the seventh day you shall rest; even in plowing time and in harvest time you shall rest.

—EXODUS 34:21

the blessing of the candles, the wine, and the children, marked the beginning of a period in which the natural order of things was restored. Just as God rested on the seventh day, so did we.

We have a Sabbath in Christian tradition as well, but as contemporary writer Lauren Winner points out, there is something missing in it for many of us.

> There is something in the Jewish Sabbath that is absent from most Christian Sundays: a true cessation from the rhythms of work and world, a time wholly set apart, and, perhaps above all, a sense that the point of Shabbat, the orientation of Shabbat, is toward God.[1]

It is that same orientation toward God that we need in the midst of transitions. God is doing something new in us, and we need to rest and watch in order to see what that new thing might be.

Be present, O merciful God, and protect us through the hours of this night, so that we who are wearied by the changes and chances of this life may rest in your eternal changelessness; through Jesus Christ our Lord. Amen.

—THE BOOK OF
COMMON PRAYER
1979

Throughout Exodus and Numbers, God insists that the Israelites rest. The first command to rest comes early in the desert journey, with the story of God providing the people with manna to eat. They are to gather it for six days, but on the sixth day they should gather enough for the seventh day as well, so they can rest on the Sabbath. Hebrew scriptures scholar Terence Fretheim notes that this command to rest "is an aspect of God's created order." This connects with the Sabbath rest that is built into the created order in Genesis 2:1–3:

> Sabbath is part of the structures of the world as a whole. . . .
> It is presented to the people (v. 23) not as a day of worship,
> but as a day of solemn rest. As such, it is an integral part of
> the life in God's new creation. By so resting, they are in tune
> with God's creational design.[2]

God repeats that command five more times in Exodus, and the theme is picked up again in Numbers, as the people continue to journey. A cloud—God—covers the tabernacle, the tent of the covenant. When the cloud lifts from the tabernacle, the people travel on. But when the cloud covers the tabernacle, the people stay put and rest. Sometimes the cloud covers the tent for a day, sometimes for a month. However long it stays there, the people are to stay in camp and refrain from moving forward (Numbers 9:15–23).

The biblical text states that the people did this in obedience to God's command, but I wonder if God did this not only to test the people's faithfulness but to give them periods of rest as well. Fretheim reminds us that God built patterns of rest and work into the very fabric of our existence.

> God's resting is a divine act that builds into the very created
> order of things a working/resting rhythm. Only when that
> rhythm is honored by all is the creation what God intended
> it to be. The sabbath is thus a divinely given means for all
> creatures to be in tune with the created order of things. Even
> more, sabbath-keeping is an act of creation-keeping.[3]

That rest—the sabbath time we need in transition—is an act of creation-keeping for us as well. And sometimes what's needed is just a day of rest; sometimes the need for sabbath time lasts for weeks or months.

I learned this for myself the first time I went on a silent and solitary retreat. I'd scheduled five days alone in a hermitage in the New Mexico desert and was more than a little anxious about what the experience might bring. As I asked people what happened on silent retreats, I got the same answer repeatedly: "You'll sleep a lot." That didn't seem very spiritual to me before the retreat, but I discovered that my friends were right. I slept a lot the first two days and rested the last three days of that retreat. And it was only by succumbing to the rest I needed that I was able to turn my attention to God and to the conversation with God that retreat time provided. Whenever I lead a retreat now, one of the first things I do is invite people to skip sessions if they need to rest. Retreat time invites us to pay attention to the need to rest, to spend time alone, or do whatever else is needed to recuperate, to get back in touch with God's working-and-resting rhythm. People often come to retreats exhausted, and more than anything, they need time to sleep and relax. Only when they've had an opportunity to do that can they be truly receptive to the ways in which God calls them to be re-created.

> *O heavenly Father, you give your children sleep for the refreshment of soul and body: Grant me this gift, I pray; keep me in that perfect peace which you have promised to those whose minds are fixed on you; and give me such a sense of your presence, that in the hours of silence I may enjoy the blessed assurance of your love; through Jesus Christ our Savior. Amen.*
>
> —THE BOOK OF COMMON PRAYER 1979

Sue Bender, a contemporary writer and artist, found this out when she spent time with the Amish. Her own journey began when some Amish quilts hanging in a store captivated her. As she went back and looked at them repeatedly, she realized that her life was more like a crazy quilt—a quilt made from lots of fabrics placed in random patterns—than the simple Amish quilts. Her life was full of choices and possibilities, and she didn't want to let go of any of them even to rest and reflect. Every day she made lists of the things to be done. "By evening," she writes, "the list had become a battlefield of hieroglyphics; crossed-off areas, checks and circles, plus the many temptations added during the day. The circles were there to remind me of all the tasks that didn't get done. Tomorrow's list began with today's leftovers."

This went on for years until finally she realized that the pace was simply too much. "Only now, looking back, can I hear a child's voice inside me calling 'STOP, I want to get off. The merry-go-round is spinning faster and faster. Please make it stop.'"[4] So Bender went and spent time with the Amish, where she learned about stopping, resting, reflecting, and letting her life be re-created.

If people need regular rest and periods of recuperation as a part of "normal" existence, imagine how much truer this is during periods of transition. Those learning to live with a chronic illness discover this quickly. A friend of mine with health problems has to stop working—stop most activity—after being up and about for twelve hours; she must rest for the next twelve if she wants to continue living. Another friend wrote me about all the wonderful conferences she wanted to attend, except they were all back-to-back, and she too has a chronic illness that flares up when she pushes herself too hard. After talking with her spiritual director, she realized that she couldn't do everything she wanted to do, even though all of it would have been enjoyable. And I have found that living with a chronic illness means I must rest more than I used to. Like it or not, my body responds poorly to being pushed beyond a certain point.

Those experiencing other kinds of transitions—divorce, the empty nest after children leave home, birth of a child, a move to a new home, place, or job—may be able to push the body harder than those with illnesses that enforce limits more dramatically, but any kind of transition exhausts us, even the transitions we've sought out. Living in the desert, traveling unfamiliar paths, involves turning off the autopilot function for a while. In the new house or apartment, we can't find the bathroom in the dark in the middle of the night. In the new city we just moved to, we can't find the peanut butter in the grocery store. After the children have all left home to live their own lives, the evenings, usually filled with activities focused on the kids, stretch out in front of parents, and it takes them a while to remember what kinds of activities were enjoyable a couple of decades ago. The same thing happens to those who've recently experienced divorce or the loss of a loved one. Transition is hard work. Newness confronts us at so many of the turns, and for many people the grief of losses jumps out at unexpected times as well. The path ahead isn't the same old well-worn, familiar one from years past. And all of that is incredibly exhausting.

Friends of mine recently adopted an eleven-year-old boy who has lived in foster homes for some time. The adoption went smoothly, with short visits between the boy and his prospective parents, followed by longer visits, placement in their home, and finally adoption. The new family worked well together, but still everyone was exhausted from months of adapting to changed circumstances. After the adoption was finalized, they all went on a cruise together—one that provided lots of activities for the young boy and lots of time for rest and relaxation for his new parents.

For my friends and for anyone in transition, finding the way ahead, charting the twists and turns of the new path, and allowing re-creation to happen takes a lot of energy. It doesn't matter if the changes are coming fast and furious and are welcome, or if it feels as though we're going nowhere fast. Rest is as necessary to the desert journey as breathing is to life.

All of this sounds rather tedious and certainly countercultural in societies where work has become an idol and exhaustion is a sign of elevated status. When I was first diagnosed with MS and discovered that I had no choice but to rest more, I couldn't imagine how I could get all my work done. What I found was that I just couldn't do everything I used to do. I know people whose illnesses prevented them from keeping their jobs or living as they always had because the tasks were just too demanding, given their new limitations. These transitions are particularly difficult, since they require such an overwhelming revamping, not only of life patterns but also of self-image or identity. Like the Egyptians, we're asked to let go of who we were in Egypt and become something new and unknown to us.

Teach us, beyond our striving,

The rich rewards of rest.

Who does not live serenely

Is never deeply blest,

O tranquil, radiant Sunlight,

Bring thou our lives to flower,

Less wearied with our effort

More aware of power.

—HARRY EMERSON FOSDICK

My own first instinct on being diagnosed with MS was to continue working hard rather than listen to my body's new limits. It took me a few months to realize that I couldn't push as hard as I had in the past, that I wasn't God and couldn't control my world at the level that I'd always thought I could. I could have used the Israelites' cloud as a guide to traveling and resting during those early days. But the signs I got were just as clear, or at least they were when I paid attention to my body, which simply wouldn't let me go as far as I wanted on any given day. More than a year later, I still struggle with keeping my workload in check some days, especially when I have to say no to things I'd really like to do.

The desert journey invites us to modify our lives, but we have to rest in order to not only hear the invitation but absorb the implications of accepting it. The Israelites stopped each time the cloud descended on the tabernacle, and in those periods of rest they had time to explore the landscape of their journey, the new surrounding. As my body enforced the needed periods of rest, I discovered that I could get the most important things done in a forty-hour workweek rather than the fifty- or sixty-hour week I'd worked for years. Some of the things that crossed my desk didn't need to be done by me (or anyone). Other members of the staff offered to help with some of the projects I'd always done. I've also discovered that what doesn't get done one day will get done on another—or not get done at all—and the world won't end.

Almighty God, teach us by your Holy Spirit, what to believe, what to do, and where to take our rest.

—DESIDERIUS ERASMUS

Sometimes it takes those transitions to force a slowdown in the schedule or to bring about a more contemplative, gentler pace that allows us to notice and appreciate what's emerging. (Remember Isaiah? "I am about to do a new thing; now it springs forth, do you not perceive it?") Rest isn't just about working less; sometimes it's about taking a break from normal activities, even activities you enjoy. In a recent interview on television, a well-known actor and director talked about how difficult it is for an actor to just stand still and do nothing in a scene. That's so much more difficult than speaking lines or being part of an action scene, he told the interviewer. It's just as hard for us to do nothing in real life. Slowing down can be like shifting gears, going from fifth to first gear without any downshifting in between. We'd rather be reading lines or performing some action stunt—doing anything!—rather than standing still, apparently doing nothing.

But the rest that seems so tedious can become a source of great liberation. Rest provides time to stop, look, and glimpse what is being created within us and consider our own part in that new creation. Even God took breaks in the creative process rather than finish everything at once. In her book on honoring our bodies, Stephanie Paulsell reminds us that God stopped and enjoyed the progress made before moving on to create some more:

> God's own work is punctuated by contemplative moments of rest, in which God gazes upon what God has made and sees that it is good. God brings light into being; God pauses to see that it is good. God creates the flowering earth; God pauses to see that it is good. God's work is not uninterrupted labor, continuous exertion. God's way of working is unrushed, thoughtful, appreciative of what is emerging.[5]

If God could take time to rest and notice, there's no reason we can't do the same. (Think about it!) In the midst of the desert, stopping for days, weeks, or even months helps us notice what new things God is about and provides the stamina to be a co-creator in the process. Pay attention to your own need for rest in the midst of transitional times. Too often, we treat ourselves like young children who keep pushing themselves long past the time when they need a nap. We become a bit like the cranky and over-tired child who won't listen to anyone and who finds everything too difficult to manage. In the midst of desert times, slow the schedule down. Take some vacation time. Reduce the demands of your schedule, even if you think that isn't possible (*especially* if you think that isn't possible). Schedule a regular sabbath day. Go on a retreat, and get away from your normal surroundings. Look up at the cloud in the sky of your own body and soul. If it's settled over the tabernacle, take a rest, get out a frozen cheesecake or whatever comfort food pleases you, and have a conversation with God for a while. Rest and look around at what God is creating and discover, as God did in Genesis, that it is good.

Make some notes in your transition journal about ways of building some regular periods of rest into your own desert time.

∿ Now I Lay Me Down to Sleep ∿

"It is in vain that you rise up early and go late to rest, eating the bread of anxious toil; for [God] gives sleep to his beloved" (Psalm 127:2).

If God gives sleep to God's beloved—all of us—why do we resist it so regularly? Most of us, according to studies, get less sleep than we should. We're so busy working and socializing during any given twenty-four-hour period that we can't find time to sleep for eight hours or more. People in transition sometimes think that if they keep busy the transition will be less painful; they won't feel so alone and won't have time to dwell on whatever distresses them. I read an article recently that advised those dealing with the anger of living with a chronic illness to stay busy as a way of keeping fear and frustration from overwhelming them. A certain amount of busyness is essential to living in transition; it can help us keep depression at bay. But keeping busy all the time only prevents progress in the desert. Sometimes—perhaps even more often in transitional times—what we need most is sleep.

> *Good Jesus, strength of the weary, rest of the restless, by the weariness and unrest of your sacred cross, come to me who am weary that I may rest in you.*
>
> —EDWARD BOUVERIE PUSEY

Take another look at the psalm that opened this section. It holds a clue about why we resist rest: vanity. To be busy—even overly busy—shows others that we're important. There's too much to get done, no time for rest. Important people can learn to do without it. To come into the office looking rested gives the impression that we're slackers, or bored, lonely people who don't have much to do. I know people who drag themselves around most days, looking utterly exhausted, proud of the fact that they only get about four or five hours of rest a night. And heaven forbid taking a nap in the middle of the day. A friend of mine, whose husband died suddenly, was surprised to discover how much sleep she's needed in her own desert time. It worried her that she could sleep ten hours a night or more until she discovered that others in her support group reported the same thing.

Sleep also frightens us at some level, consciously or unconsciously. That's why the Compline service—the traditional last service of the evening before bed in monasteries—is full of prayers that beg God to keep the demons at bay. "Be our light in the darkness, O Lord, and in your great mercy defend us from all perils and dangers this night. . . ." "Visit this place, O Lord, and drive far from it all snares of the enemy . . . ," say two of the prayers from The Book of Common Prayer's Compline service. Even the most common of children's prayers acknowledges our fear of the dark and of death: "Now I lay me down to sleep. I pray the Lord my soul to keep. If I should die before I wake. . . ."

"The Lord Almighty grant us a peaceful night and a perfect end," are words that begin the Episcopal service of Compline. Equating a peaceful night tonight and a perfect end to life, something we do over and over in nighttime prayers—that's scary and a natural fear. Darkness—closing our eyes and trusting that nothing bad will happen while we're not watching—requires trust. But in transition especially, allowing ourselves to be re-created means commending our spirits to God and giving God the lead. It means trusting that nothing is impossible with God, even what seems ridiculous or crazy.

We have to learn to befriend whatever frightens us about the night—and about transitions in general—as a traditional Franciscan story reminds us. In a quiet little village where nothing much ever happened, the villagers woke up one morning to find the night watchman dead, lying in a pool of his own blood. A wolf had attacked and killed the man. The people were terrified and called on a wise hermit who lived just outside of town. Some of them wanted the hermit to kill the wolf; others wanted the hermit to tame it. Still other people wanted the hermit to show them how to build high fences around the village to keep all dangers out. The hermit, being truly wise, said he would do what he could. So he went out into the woods and met with the wolf.

He came back later that day, and the people anxiously asked him what he had done to solve their problem. "It's very simple," he told them. "Just feed the wolf and you'll have no more problems."

The villagers thought the hermit was crazy, and they all went home and locked themselves in for the night. Later, though, as they heard the wolf prowling the city, each household cracked the door just a little and pushed a bowl of food out for the wolf. Night after night they discovered that if they left food for the wolf, it wouldn't hurt anyone. By tending—feeding—what scared them in the night, they became friends with it, and it no longer harmed them. The same is true of whatever frightens us. Running from it only gives it more power over us. Confronting it, feeding it, can turn our fears into companions.

Sometimes people fear sleep because God seems to have more access to us during the night than during daylight hours. When we're busy and otherwise occupied, God may find it difficult to break in for some conversation. Keeping God at bay is easier when tasks and busy schedules occupy all the time available. But at night, as many people in the Bible found out, God seems to have less fettered access to us, particularly through dreams.

Helpful dreams have accompanied many transitions in my own life. In the midst of one transitional time, I dreamed of my current life in black-and-white, and then, half-way through the dream, I wandered into a beautiful garden, filled with brightly colored flowers. I woke up knowing that I was about to enter a new stage of my life, even if I didn't yet know what that stage was about. But the colorful garden in my dream left me hopeful about what was ahead rather than anxious.

Keep watch, dear Lord, with those who work, or watch, or weep this night, and give your angels charge over those who sleep. Tend the sick, Lord Christ; give rest to the weary, bless the dying, soothe the suffering, pity the afflicted, shield the joyous; and all for your love's sake. Amen.

—THE BOOK OF COMMON PRAYER 1979

You may find that you remember more of your dreams in the desert or that your dreams are more vivid. Remembering them and looking at them more closely can help in discerning the roadmap ahead.

If you've never kept track of your dreams, try this:

- Keep your transition journal and a pen or pencil by the bedside and record dreams whenever they wake you. Just write down whatever you remember, whether it makes sense or not.
- When you're fully awake the next day, consider those dreams more carefully.

You might find it helpful to settle yourself in a quiet place
and re-live the dream, asking God to fill in the gaps or to
help make the meaning of the dream clear.

- Pay attention to the feelings that the dream brings about
in you. Did the dream leave you feeling relaxed and hopeful, or anxious and worried? Those feelings—whatever
they are—sometimes provide clues about the dream's
meaning.

- If you're not sure what the dream points to, try talking to
a trusted friend or spiritual director who might be able
help you understand how God may be speaking to you
through dreams.

Some churches, retreat centers, and other institutions offer
dream groups to join, to give participants practice in the art of
interpreting dreams. Sometimes the simple process of telling someone about your dream or writing about it in a journal helps
uncover the dream's wisdom.

One warning about dreams in the midst of transitions:
occasionally in the transition process, active or disturbing dreams
come too often or too vividly and disrupt sleep. A wise spiritual
director taught me to pray to God to take the dreams away for a
little while when this happens. God cares about what we need and
knows when deep sleep, instead of enlightenment, is needed.
When I've prayed to be free of dreams for a bit, I find I can sleep
soundly for a time. The dreams return when I am rested and
ready to pay attention again.

There are lots of reasons people in transition resist sleep, consciously or unconsciously. Look at your own resistance to sleep if
you find yourself staying up too late or waking up for hours in the
middle of the night. Sometimes a medical condition causes insom-
nia, and anyone with difficulty sleeping is wise to check with a

medical professional or a sleep disorder clinic about possible solutions. Check the conditions for sleeping in your bedroom as well. Is it dark enough? Comfortable enough? Quiet enough? People with difficulty sleeping sometimes find it helpful to create a routine around bedtime. Going to sleep and rising at roughly the same time each day helps some people. So does a bedtime ritual, such as a warm bath before bed, reading for a little while before sleeping, or using relaxing scents on the pillow or in the air. But if the problem stems from a resistance to sleep— to letting go of the controls in order to sleep—prayer may be part of the answer. Many prayer books today feature evening, or Compline, services that help us pray through the fears of letting go of the reins and of our fear of death.

 Return, O my soul, to your rest, for the LORD has dealt bountifully with you.

For you have delivered my soul from death, my eyes from tears, my feet from stumbling.

I walk before the LORD in the land of the living.

—PSALM 116:7–9

Find a bedtime prayer service that seems to speak to your own fears and make a habit of praying it each night, right before bedtime.

Consider using the last line of the psalm quoted at the beginning of this chapter as a reminder that sleep is a gift from God. As you lie down for the night, repeat the line, "God gives sleep to his beloved," over and over as you breathe gently, and remember that you are one of God's beloved. Many people find it helpful to keep some prayer beads or a rosary near their bed. Reciting a line like the psalm just quoted or some other piece of scripture or a comforting thought, while fingering the beads one by one, can be a powerful aid to sleeping and knowing that we are wrapped in God's arms as we do so.

∿ Cut It Out ∿

Taking care of ourselves in the midst of transition isn't always a matter of resting or getting more sleep. Sometimes it's just a matter of doing less. But if you find yourself not wanting to do *any-thing*—like getting out of bed in the morning, seeing friends, and going about the normal daily things—that may be depression rather than just fatigue during a time of transition; help from a doctor or other health-care professional could be in order. But almost all transitions require some adjustment of the pace of life. The Israelites certainly didn't race through the hot desert.

Desert times also ask us to let go of the familiar, or at least some of it. The Israelites took some familiar things with them as they left Egypt. They also went as an entire community, a support system for one another. But in the desert, they also had to learn new skills, find new resources, and develop different relationships with each other. No longer slaves, they had to learn to live without overseers and relate to each other without the Egyptian structures imposed upon them. Desert time is about blending some of what is familiar and comfortable with space for the unknown and new to enter in.

A very competent friend of mine was downsized from her job last year. She had worked with my organization before, and I was trying to fill a position at work at that time—one for which she would have been perfect. We spent some time talking about the position, but she was wiser than I was at the time. She'd been given outplacement services as she looked for a new job, and in working with that service she discovered that she wasn't sure what she wanted to do next in life or where she wanted to head long term. So she decided to stay with the process of discerning where God was calling her, sticking with the transition process, even though she could have had a job that would have ended her time in the desert. She was wise enough to realize that she had the time, support systems, and financial resources to live in the desert for a while and look at that time as creative time rather than drudgery or exile. She didn't jump into a position just because it was familiar to her. That required courage on her part. Taking the job could have put her back on autopilot in comfortable territory, but she would have lost the opportunity (at least at that moment) to explore the unfamiliar and perhaps find a treasure in the process.

 The LORD is my shepherd, I shall not want.

He makes me lie down in green pastures; he leads me beside still waters;

he restores my soul. He leads me in right paths for his name's sake.

Parker Palmer, a wonderful educator, writer, and speaker, provides another example of someone cutting his schedule back deliberately in order to create time to walk through the desert with God for a while. At a recent conference, he announced that he was about to turn sixty-five— a significant birthday— and that he planned to

Even though I walk through the darkest valley, I fear no evil; for you are with me; your rod and your staff—they comfort me.

You prepare a table before me in the presence of my enemies; you anoint my head with oil; my cup overflows.

Surely goodness and mercy shall follow me all the days of my life, and I shall dwell in the house of the LORD my whole life long.

—PSALM 23

take a year off to rest and reevaluate where he was in life. He would take an entire year off in order to ponder what else he needed to do in this life and wasn't accepting any future speaking engagements or projects until that year was over. He was planning a sabbatical year, essentially, one in which he would cease his normal activities and take time to rest, listen, and be re-created.

I found time off like this invaluable in my own life as well and am trying to make sure I get some of this kind of time each year. About a year ago, I was exhausted after an extremely busy period of time—one in which I had been traveling and leading retreats and speaking at conferences almost nonstop for four months. Because my illness had been diagnosed only a couple of months before my busy and already-scheduled travels began, I was even more exhausted than I would have been had I been perfectly healthy. About three months into the travel season, I began to notice how worn I was, how irritable I was getting, and how deeply I needed rest.

So I scheduled two months for myself with the lightest possible schedule. I made few plans for that time. I didn't even plan social events. For two summer months I tended to the work at my office, saw a few friends, and went to a movie here and there. But mostly when I wasn't working I spent time only with people very close to me, people who didn't need anything from me but my presence. I read novels, slept late on weekends, took naps and walks, and recuperated. I knew there was a heavy workload coming up in September, and I was tempted to start in on it over the summer to lighten September's load, but I didn't. I rested. And I finally had some time to think about the illness with which I'd been diagnosed, to think about what kind of life I needed to live if this was going to be an ongoing part of my reality. I had time to catch glimpses of and get used to my new existence. Maybe the Israelites had the same experience when the cloud over the tabernacle kept them in place for weeks or months at a time. Perhaps that time out gave them an opportunity to begin exploring what it meant to be the people of God instead of slaves.

Doing less is difficult, however, because being busy is often a status symbol. Saying no when you don't have other plans or a good excuse, especially when you could do what's being asked of you, is difficult. Think back to the bind Moses got himself in by being busy all the time. Rather than say no or delegate tasks to others, Moses ignored his limits, thinking he could do it all himself—and that he *should* do it all.

That word *should* gets most of us into all kinds of trouble. It seems to have a magical power, maybe harking back to childhood images of a parent or authority figure telling us what we "should" do. Years ago a friend of mine gave me a great line that I've used ever since: "Don't should on yourself," she used to say. Saying no when we need time to rest, recuperate, and be re-created is particularly difficult if you're should-ing on yourself. But in the midst of the desert journey, it helps to learn how to use the word *no*, to cut back as my friend did, and as Parker Palmer and Moses did, in order to focus on the desert path for a time. In some ways saying no is actually about deepening whatever restlessness our hearts feel in the desert. Or perhaps saying no and doing less simply amplifies the restless voice within and gives us the time to identify that voice as God. And to listen.

It may be helpful to remember that oftentimes we find that we're more uncomfortable with saying no than people are with getting no from us. Those who know us well, or even know just the circumstances of our journey, usually understand that breathing space and a break from the routine is necessary.

Find a quiet time and place to spend a little time thinking about the "shoulds" and "ought-to's" in your life. Think back to the story of Jethro and Moses that was explored in the previous chapter (Exodus 18:13–27). Sit quietly for a few minutes and think back over the last few days or longer, looking for the times when you felt like you should

*do something or when you felt like saying no and were uncomfortable
with that.*

- Write a list of the times that the shoulds and ought-to's
  were strong for you, as well as your feelings at the time.
  Did the shoulds and ought-to's come from someone you
  know? From within you? Are they old voices from your
  past, rather than ones from a current situation?
- Imagine having a conversation with one of the shoulds or
  ought-to's on your list. Invite it to talk with you and make
  its case, but be sure to make your case for whatever you
  need right now as well. Can you work out a truce with
  the people or voices from the past who are giving you bad
  advice right now?
- What's the worst thing that could happen if you didn't listen to the shoulds and ought-to's right now? What's the
  best thing that could happen if you didn't listen? Record
  your thoughts in your journal.

∿ Doing More ∿

"Do I contradict myself?" wrote poet Walt Whitman in *Leaves of
Grass*. Yes, came back his answer to his own question. And I'm
going to do a little of that myself by making a suggestion that is
diametrically opposed to the one I just made. Sometimes you need
to do less, but sometimes you need to do more, as long as it's more
of the right things.

So many people lead sedentary lives these days that many of
us could do with more exercise. We need to rest from sitting still.
Exercise brings about feelings of relaxation and peacefulness, helps
sharpen thought processes, both of which help people sleep and
manage the stress of transitions better.

The issue of exercising doesn't arise in the Exodus stories, since the Israelites were in constant motion. The Israelites who left Egypt were slaves, people very used to manual work. After years of heavy labor, they walked—for years—in the desert. Moses didn't need to organize aerobics, karate, or yoga classes for these people, though Miriam did get them dancing once in a while (Exodus 15:20–21). The Israelites used their bodies all the time. They walked, they built things, and they gathered manna to eat six days a week. They didn't need to be encouraged to use their bodies in the midst of their transition; they had no choice.

> *Do you not know that your body is a temple of the Holy Spirit?*
>
> —1 CORINTHIANS 6:19

Today most people have a choice about exercising. The current problem with obesity in the United States indicates that too often we choose a sedentary existence instead of an active one. We are called to care for our bodies all the time, but especially during transitional times. "Do you not know that your body is a temple of the Holy Spirit?" wrote Paul in 1 Corinthians 6:19. We are the stewards—the caretakers—for the bodies that we live in, and bodies need as much care as souls during times of transition. Exercise helps fight off feelings of depression, fatigue, and hopelessness and increases the ability to be receptive to God's presence.

One of the challenges of living with MS for me was learning to exercise regularly. Early on I discovered that what my doctor had told me was true: most of the time I felt tired and didn't have the energy to exercise. The more tired I got, the more I ignored exercise, which only exacerbated the problems. Without exercise I found I was experiencing both fatigue and physical restlessness at the same time.

About six months into the desert time of learning to live with MS, I began walking, just a mile at first, and even that challenged me. But I kept it up and made myself walk a mile three times a week. As my energy levels rose, I extended some of my walks or walked more often. When winter came, I got a videotaped program so I could walk indoors.

For health and food,

For love and friends,

For everything

Thy goodness sends,

Father in Heaven,

We thank Thee.

—RALPH WALDO
EMERSON

Walking wasn't a cure-all. I still had days when I felt very tired, but there were fewer of them. And as the fatigue subsided, I found myself feeling less overwhelmed and more hopeful. I was reminded of wisdom I'd temporarily lost track of: bodies and minds are inseparable. Care for the body, and you're caring for the soul and mind as well.

Movement—feeling the blood coursing through the veins and adrenalin in the system—just plain feels good after you get past the beginning stages. And movement can take all sorts of forms. Walking, swimming, or a class that teaches yoga, tai chi, or other kinds of exercise, with the added benefit of community, can be a real gift in transitional times, as long as it's movement that's appropriate to your physical health and limitations. Movement isn't a happiness pill of some sort. Walking for forty years didn't turn the Israelites into a chipper bunch. But God gave us remarkable bodies that bring with them all kinds of marvelous sensations and responses.

Depending on your own physical condition, seek out some form of exercise or physical movement that you'll enjoy. Choose an exercise program that is appropriate to your needs and abilities. Those facing new physical challenges in their lives and those who have been inactive for long periods of time should consult their health-care professional about appropriate exercise levels before commencing any program. If you're not taking a class with others, finding a partner to exercise with can be helpful, not only for the companionship but for the accountability. Find something you enjoy doing and practice it regularly. You may be surprised how much different the desert looks when you're walking through it, as the Israelites did, than when you're being sedentary and waiting for it to pass.

～ Food and Faith ～

"The people of God do not live by bread alone," writes Fretheim, "but they cannot live without bread either. God's new creation is more than a spiritual matter; it is a comprehensive reality, effecting change in every nook and cranny of the world's life, including people's everyday needs."[6] And one of the most basic needs people have is food. We must eat in order to live. In the midst of transition, sometimes we must eat differently than we used to, but eat we must.

Food and water—and the lack of them—was a regular complaint of the Israelites. In fact, the theme of food, or nourishment, wends its way throughout the Exodus stories. God provides food repeatedly. The laws that God gives to the people concern the food they'll eat. God even instructs the

In the evening quails came up and covered the camp; and in the morning there was a layer of dew around the camp. When the layer of dew lifted, there on the surface of the wilderness was a fine flaky substance, as fine as frost on the ground. When the Israelites saw it, they said to one another, "What is it?" For they did not know what it was. Moses said to them, "It is the bread that the LORD has given you to eat.

—EXODUS 16:13–16

Israelites to celebrate their harvests, both the first fruits of the harvest and the ingathering of the harvest at the end of the year (Exodus 23:16–17). God intends that we have the food, water, and nourishment that we need. And that's so important that God instructs Moses to keep a little of the manna on display:

> "This is what the LORD has commanded" Moses tells the people. "Let an omer of it be kept throughout your generations, in order that they may see the food with which I fed you in the wilderness, when I brought you out of the land of Egypt." And Moses said to Aaron, "Take a jar, and put an omer of manna in it, and place it before the LORD, to be kept throughout your generations" (Exodus 16:32–33).

The number of laws God gives about food also indicates that God cares not only *that* we eat but cares about *what* we eat. For the Jewish people, especially those of the Orthodox Jewish tradition, that means eating *kosher*—or, as Lauren Winner tells us, fitting food—food of which God approves. That sounds like a diet to most of us, but Winner shares the difference between keeping kosher and going on a diet:

> At its most basic level, keeping kosher requires you to be present to your food. Of course, so does the Atkins diet. The difference between Atkins and *kashrut* [kosher eating] is God. We try out the Atkins diet because our physician cares about what we eat. We limit ourselves to kosher food . . . because God cares about what we eat.[7]

Transitions sometimes require us to modify our eating habits, too, to be present to our food and the nourishment obtained from it. For some people that means leaving behind unhealthy food or drink. The alcoholic has to give up liquor if she wants to journey toward recovery. The man with heart problems has to give up eating high-fat desserts each evening and learn to enjoy fruits and vegetables. For other people the journey involves learning to eat again, rather than eating differently. The girl who wants to recover from bulimia has to learn to tolerate food and to treat food as the gift from God that it is rather than as the enemy.

People dealing with depression or anger—emotions common in transitional times—sometimes need to remember to eat at all. Both emotions can drive hunger far from the mind, but forgetting or choosing not to eat only makes matters worse. Look at how cranky the Israelites got when they didn't have the food or water they wanted. I've had to battle this occasionally myself, particularly around work issues. When I'm overstressed and the workload is too heavy, I tend to just keep working and "forget" to eat. That's sometimes my way of wearing myself out even further so others will see how hard I'm working and take pity on me, but it rarely evokes the sympathy I'm looking for.

I subscribe to a magazine about organic living, and one of the things they've been touting recently is the slow-food movement. The movement is all about getting fresh food and cooking a meal that takes longer to prepare than the usual five minutes in the microwave. It's about preparing and eating good food, usually in the company of others. Fundamentally, the slow-food movement celebrates the

 God is great, and God is good,
And we thank God for our food,
By God's hand we all are fed;
Thank you, Lord, for our daily bread.

—Author unknown

gift of food. It also celebrates food that is in season, rather than strawberries flown in from distant shores in the dead of winter.

That speaks to me in the midst of transition. What can I eat that is in season—the season of the year, as well as the season of my own transformation—that will be nourishing? What kind of food, eaten thoughtfully, nourishes the body God gave me so I can continue on the journey?

Nowhere has food as a gift from God—one that nourishes body and soul—been portrayed so powerfully as in the movie "Babette's Feast." If you've never seen it, the movie is available from most video stores. A young woman comes to live in a very austere community, where food is spare, almost tasteless. Unbeknownst to the community, this woman was a famous chef in her native France. One day she wins the lottery and decides to use the money to put on an extraordinary feast for those who've taken her in. She orders all sorts of wondrous foods from distant shores, much to the consternation of the ascetic community of which she's a part. Though the townsfolk agree to come to her meal, they decide they won't enjoy it, no matter what. But the gift of her food, the gracious presentation, the delightful smells, sights, and tastes win them over. They can't help but be delighted with the food and, in spite of themselves, come to understand the meal as Communion.

"The gifts of God for the people of God," says the priest in my own tradition when she raises the bread and wine at the Eucharist. For Christians the bread and the wine are the body and blood of Christ—a gift from God—but it is still bread and wine that we eat and drink. God wants to nourish us and does so with these commonplace foods: simple bread and the juice of some grapes.

For Christians, Jews, and others, food is a gift from God. The juiciness of the apple, the tartness of the lemon, the pungent smell of rosemary or garlic, the sweetness of chocolate—these are gifts to be treasured (especially that chocolate!). More than that, food—the right kind and in the right amounts—is fuel for the journey. It keeps us going, or at least doing as much as possible.

Like rest and exercise, eating well—whatever that means for each of us—is a way of helping our bodies and souls move forward in the journey. If the transition you're experiencing is a medical one, a health care provider may be able to provide invaluable help about what foods and eating cycles or times will be most helpful. Think of your physician's, nurse's, or nutritionist's advice as the law God provided the Israelites, and try to adjust eating habits as necessary. Even if your transition isn't related to health, practice treating food as a gift from God and discover ways of cherishing it. Make meals a time for good food, cooked well, and community. Set a beautiful table for yourself sometimes, whether you're eating alone or with others. Practice being attentive to the food you eat and the gifts it provides—the energy, comfort, and sensory satisfaction. Eat, but eat well. Eat fitting food that sustains you on the journey.

CHAPTER V

Are We There Yet?

*There are graces, we all come to realize, that we'd
rather not receive. Theologians used to distinguish
between special grace and common grace, but we've
never much valued the latter. Special grace is
extraordinary; it comes with drama and flair. We are
rescued, singled out in a momentous act of boldness.
But common grace falls upon the just and unjust alike.
It strikes us as simply too . . . ordinary.*[1]
—BELDEN LANE

The diagnosis of multiple sclerosis came with that odd combination of drama and nondrama that's so characteristic of transitions. My doctor called to give me the results of the MRI in the middle of a staff meeting. I went ahead and took the call while my colleagues conversed among themselves. "We found some lesions in your brain," he told me. "OK," I thought, still focused on the staff meeting. The doctor continued: "These kinds of lesions can indicate that a stroke is coming, but we don't think that's the case. The other possibility is that you have multiple sclerosis, which seems likely. I want you to see a neurologist."

I already knew a little about MS from a friend whose daughter had been diagnosed with it. It was more serious than a head cold but a lot less serious than some other diagnoses. My doctor and I discussed the details of setting up a neurology appointment and ended the conversation. I went back to my staff meeting.

About an hour later, the reality of the diagnosis set in. As is often true with sudden shocks, the information took a while to register. This was a big deal, even if it wasn't life-threatening. I count myself fortunate to have known of people who lived quite comfortably with MS. That knowledge cushioned the blow when I got my own diagnosis. But I also knew others who didn't live so easily with it. MS seriously disables some people, and no crystal ball could tell me whether my future lay in the first group or the latter one, or somewhere in between.

Without a final and definitive diagnosis, I worked hard at accepting the possibility of living with MS, but I also put it at arm's length for the time being. I called it "not buying trouble." It's so easy to create "what-if" scenarios when the news might be scary, and I tried hard to avoid frightening myself with images of the worst possible future. It seemed like a good strategy at the time, and it certainly helped me get through the months that followed, when there weren't many clear answers. Subsequent neurology visits and tests confirmed the MS diagnosis. Getting the actual diagnosis and learning to give myself injections was hard, but I got through all of it with the help of friends and medical professionals.

 Be merciful to me, O God, be merciful to me, for in you my soul takes refuge; in the shadow of your wings I will take refuge, until the destroying storms pass by.

—PSALM 57:1

After a few months of high drama, life settled back down to something rather ordinary. I was regularly more tired than I used to be. There were some side effects from the injections, but nothing dramatic or unmanageable. Like the Israelites after crossing the Red Sea, I found myself in desert time without a clear path—or even clear danger—ahead of me. After the intense focus on tests and learning new procedures, the time ahead looked a bit, well, boring. It wasn't exactly that I wanted to return to the weeks of high drama that had held my focus for so long. But at least the drama had given me something to do. What was I supposed to do now?

In his book *The Solace of Fierce Landscapes*, Belden Lane describes a similar experience when dealing with his mother's diagnosis of cancer. He steeled himself to be the faithful son at his mother's deathbed. The only problem was she didn't die as quickly as everyone expected. Her cancer went into remission, but Alzheimer's set in. Life for him became routine visits to his mother's nursing home, waiting for something to happen. He writes,

> Difficult as it was, at first, to discern grace in the grotesque,
> it became even more difficult to discover grace in the pro-
> longed redundancy of ordinariness. How could I adjust to
> life's untheatrical regularity when I'd been prepared for

grand opera and dark tragedy? . . . How would I deal with
the uneventful and commonplace? . . . I needed a spirituality of the uneventful, of the low places in one's life that are
neither deep nor exhilaratingly high.[2]

Most transitions could benefit from a "spirituality of the
uneventful." Life in the desert so often lacks definition or focus.
It's life without high or low points for the most part. The sun rises
and sets. Sand stretches out endlessly. Nothing much seems to be
happening. Like the Israelites, we're looking at a long, roundabout
path stretched out ahead, but where are the directional signs? A
friend of mine visited a museum recently and saw an exhibit with
sand in an enclosed case and a button you could push to change
the direction of the wind within the case. With the touch of that
button, the whole desert landscape changed. "I thought about how
unaware you would be of the massive landscape change if you were
actually in the midst of it," she wrote me.

> The shifting of the sands would not seem so dramatic to
> you and you would only see a bit of what was in front of
> you rather than the whole thing. I wonder if the Holy Spirit
> blowing through our lives in the midst of transition isn't a
> bit like this. Our entire spiritual landscape may be shifting,
> but we don't see the whole picture and may not think any-
> thing is changing at all.[3]

Traveling through the desert, I want a sign that says:
"Canaan: 197 miles." Something definitive and clear. But sign-
posts, if they're there at all, are infrequent, and the distance
between oases can be astounding. And that assumes that you know
where you're going in the first place.

All of that can make transitions tedious and frustrating.
They're not orderly. The path isn't straight or well marked. All too

often the path looks endless as well, as it did for Belden Lane sitting at his mother's side. And that's enough to make most of us crazy, partly—(and oddly enough) from boredom, which frequently brings its companions: restlessness, anxiety, fear, and frustration.

Miriam Therese Winter, a professor at Hartford Seminary, writes of the angst of that experience of wandering without clear focus in the desert in a psalm she wrote based on the life of Moses' wife, Zipporah, who journeyed in the desert with Moses.

> *Promise us,*
> *O God of the Exodus,*
> *promise You will keep*
> *Your promise,*
> *for the land we seek*
> *seems far from us*
> *and the road we travel*
> *is long.*
> *Promise we will come*
> *to the promised land*
> *while we can still remember*
> *the vision and the traditions*
> *to which we once belonged.*
> *Amen.*[4]

"Promise us. . . ." Winters has Zipporah saying over and over again. Promise us you'll keep up your end of the bargain, God, and bring us to a new home. Promise us we'll get there before we forget who we are and why we started (or were sent) on this journey in the first place. The words are plaintive—ones I can identify with in my own experience of transitions. "Are we there yet?" we want to know, just like the child on a long road trip with her parents. And that question is all the more frustrating when we don't know what "there" will be when we get there. Though what we need is Lane's spirituality of the uneventful, most of us would rather just get "there" so we won't need to learn to live with God in uneventful times at all. But as Lane writes from his own experience of the desert: "Only at the periphery of our lives, where we and our understanding of God alike are undone, can we understand bewilderment as occasioning another way of knowing."[5]

O God, by whom the meek are guided in judgment, and light rises up in darkness for the godly; give us, in all our doubts and uncertainties the grace to ask what thou wouldst have us do; that the spirit of wisdom may save us from all false choices, and that in thy light we may see light and in thy straight path may not stumble; through Jesus Christ our Lord.

—WILLIAM BRIGHT

Bewilderment, the process of being undone, of restlessness, of not being able to live the way we used to live but being without a vision—or even a clue—of how to live now—turns out to be a gift in the desert. Not knowing where we are, when we will get "there," or what the new land will look like are invitations to practice a spirituality of the uneventful.

∿ Doin' Nothin', Nothin' Doin' ∿

The spouse whose partner has died gets through the arrangements for burial and the funeral all right, but it's the weeks, months, and years ahead that stretch out as empty space that prove the most difficult. It's the nights alone, after all the friends and family have moved on with their lives that are the hardest.

Mom and Dad send their last child off to college. But after a few nights of peace and quiet, they discover that so much of their time was spent working around the kids' schedules all those years that they've forgotten what they used to do before the kids arrived.

Or the middle-aged man who had a career in construction now sits in a wheelchair—a permanent addition to his life as the result of a car accident—and wonders what he'll do, now that he can't climb up steel girders anymore.

In one of these spaces where we don't know what's ahead or where to turn, the first instinct is usually to do something—any-thing! "Idle hands are the devil's workshop," I was told in my

 Arise, O sun of righteousness, upon us, with healing in thy wings; make us children of the light and of the day. Show us the way in which we should walk, for unto thee, O Lord, do we lift up our souls.

—THOMAS SHERLOCK

growing-up years. Doing something is always better than doing nothing. It's not hard to identify with the foolish lengths we some-times go to in order to keep busy, just like the man in this old joke. A man found his neighbor on his hands and knees in the yard one day, looking for his keys. The kind man offered to help his neigh-bor and got down on his own hands and knees and searched. After quite a while, when neither of them had found anything, the neigh-bor asked his friend where he'd lost the keys. "At home," the man replied. "Then why are we searching here in the yard?" the aston-ished neighbor asked. "Because it's brighter here," the man replied.[6]

Belden Lane tells a similar story. After a delightful walk in unfamiliar woods one day, he headed back to his cabin. But he got lost, and it was quite a while before the sound of a car on a nearby road helped him find his way back. "I should have stopped and calmly paid attention to where I was," Lane writes. [But] "this is a mask of what I've done so often in my life; suspecting I'm on the wrong path, I go faster in hopes of proving it to be the right one after all."[7]

It's easy to identify with the man who was searching for his keys in the wrong place because the light was better and with Lane's need to go faster when he's lost. Doing something, even something utterly futile, making progress, getting things done, demonstrating results—those are valued activities. Doing nothing, being indecisive, admitting that we don't know what's next or how far the walk will be or what "there" is—well, that's for the weak or the lazy.

> *Father, I am seeing: I am hesitant and uncertain. But will you, O God, watch over each step of mine and guide me.*
>
> —ST. AUGUSTINE

Only it's not. *Something* is happening, even when we're not aware of it. In *Nothing Ever Happens on My Block,* Ellen Raskin's charming book for children, Chester Filbert sits on the curb in front of his house and complains endlessly about how quiet his street is in comparison to other people's blocks. He imagines parades, haunted houses, courageous acts of various sorts happening on other blocks, but nothing ever happens on his. Chester, however, sits with his back to his neighborhood throughout the whole book, and in the pictures behind him kids play practical jokes on adults, police capture robbers, a young girl breaks her leg and gets taken away in an ambulance, a parachutist drops in, and so on.[8]

The book, as is so often true of good children's books, speaks a truth about life in general. Even when it seems as if nothing is happening, that's not usually the case. People who are learning to make prayer a part of their daily life often grapple with the sense that nothing is happening. After the initial rush that comes with learning something new, routine sets in. What felt very exciting the first week or two becomes repetitive and boring. New skills, like the initial stage of transitions, bring with them excitement and drama, at least at some level. They engage us, even if the transition is painful. But then the routine (or the new routine) sets in, the drama disappears, and nothing seems to be happening.

Sue Monk Kidd speaks poignantly in *When the Heart Waits* of the confusion she felt when she found herself in transition. As she realized that her own sense of identity was changing, she writes about that part of the process when she's neither what she was nor what she wants to be, and about her desire to fix things, to be one thing or the other, rather than journeying through the desert:

> I felt inward pressure to change, yet I also felt pressure to remain the same. I got anxious over the way my old identity was losing its contours. A part of me wanted to shore it up as a child would pat a crumbling creation in a sandbox. Another part of me wanted to shed the old identity too quickly. No more Little Girl with a Curl, no more Little Red Hen, no more Tin Woodman. Peel them off like skin. I want out![9]

Most of us would do just about anything to dispense with that part of the journey. There has to be a way to get where we're going right now, or at least to fix the journey so it's more interesting, more productive along the way. Maybe that's why Moses kept himself so busy settling all the disputes for the Israelites until Jethro got him to stop and let go of the reins. At one level, it was probably easier for Moses to spend entire days settling disputes and trying to fix things than to stare at unstructured time without clear answers and responsibilities.

"In keeping with our mechanistic bias, we have tried to make do with recharging and repair," writes William Bridges in his book on transitions, "imagining that renewal comes through fixing something defective or supplying something that is missing."[10] We summon our strength or whatever we need to get through a crisis, just as the Israelites did when leaving Egypt and escaping the Egyptians. But what happens after that? As with the Israelites, it's easy to grow impatient with periods in which there is nothing to be done. It's instinct to want to fix something, supply something, do anything, when what there is to do is precisely *nothing*. It's only by letting go of the need to control the situation—by doing nothing—that we find the energy needed to discern which way to go next.

> *Lift up our souls, O Lord, to the pure, serene light of thy presence; that there we may breathe freely, there repose in thy love, there may be at rest from ourselves, and from thence return, arraying in thy peace, to do and be what shall please thee; for thy holy name's sake.*
>
> —EDWARD BOUVERIE PUSEY

A friend of mine, who is in the midst of a sabbatical from her work, finds herself in something of a desert space at the moment—a time when she's realizing that her own priorities may not match with those that her work environment encourages. She was offered a very attractive, high-powered job recently. But as she thought about it, she realized that accepting that job might only take her further from what she really loves doing. She wisely decided to take the next year to wait, listen, and discern what she feels most deeply called to do and be, to sit in the desert deliberately and not make big decisions suddenly. She's going to sit on the curb, let go of the controls, and see what speaks to her over the next year. She's also found that taking time—even up to an hour some days—for silence, for doing nothing, has been incredibly nourishing.

It can be difficult for some people to find time for being silent and doing nothing, particularly in a household with others, especially children. But doing nothing—practicing silence—is essential to making it through the desert in a sane fashion. Even if you can only find five or ten minutes a day, it is important to develop a practice of silent listening, to stop long enough in the desert to hear what God may be calling out of you.

If this is a new practice to you, try the following:

- Find a space in your home or somewhere convenient to you that feels like sacred space. It needs to be a comfortable spot, preferably one that is quiet and solitary, that feels safe and holy to you.
- If the space is in your home (rather than a park bench, for instance), you may find it helpful to put a comfortable chair in the space and any objects that feel sacred to you. Candles, icons, photographs, prayer shawls, and other objects that signify what is holy and comforting to you will make the space more of a prayer space. Avoid a space where phones, doorbells, and other distractions happen regularly.
- Commit to spending a period of time in that space regularly, daily if possible. It doesn't need to be a long period of time. If five minutes a day is all you can manage, that's fine.
- Go to your space, and invite God to be very present to you during the time you spend there. Open your own heart to God, asking that you be enabled to hear as clearly as possible during your prayer time.
- Either sit quietly, or if it is more contemplative for you, walk around your space, deliberately clearing your mind of whatever distracts you from being with God.

- Focusing on your breathing or repeating a sacred word to yourself can help empty your mind of the daily to-do lists and whatever else is there.
- Spend your time in this space just speaking whatever is on your heart to God, paying attention to however God may be present to you, and listening to whatever you might hear. Don't worry if you aren't hearing any response on a given day, or series of days. This isn't unusual. As much as possible, remember that God is present and concerned for your welfare, and trust that, in time, the answers you need will become clear.

This kind of practice isn't a quick fix. You won't get magic answers by the end of a week. But the regular practice of silence—making space for the conversation with God—will gradually increase your own ability to hear God's voice in your life.

∿ Who Are You? ∿

In an episode of one of my favorite television shows, *Star Trek: The Next Generation,* Troi, the ship's counselor, suffers night after night from a lack of sleep. She goes to bed each night and goes to sleep, but her dreams are interrupted before she can reach a REM sleep state, so she wakes up more exhausted each day. Finally, she realizes that something—or someone—is trying to get her attention. With the help of the ship's doctor, she finds a way to confront the alien being who's disturbing her sleep. Under the doctor's supervision, she goes to sleep and comes face-to-face with the being again. "Who are you?" she asks it, and finally gets the answers she needs. That's the kind of "doing nothing" that's required in the midst of transition.

Doing nothing doesn't entail sitting alone in a silent room waiting ceaselessly, any more than it involves sitting on the curb, like Chester Filbert, moaning about how boring life is, although anyone living in the desert is entitled to do at least a little moaning and groaning. "Doing nothing," despite the sound of that phrase, is an active process. As it was for Troi in *Star Trek,* doing nothing involved confronting whatever it was that demanded her attention and asking it who it was and what it wanted. Doing nothing in the desert is about connecting with God, about listening, paying attention, and watching for what's trying to be born. Like Troi, we have to summon the courage and energy to turn to whatever is trying to get our attention and ask it who it is and what it wants.

In *A Place Like Any Other,* contemporary writer Molly Wolf wrote of a time in her life when she was unable even to focus on a game of gin rummy—a problem not uncommon in the midst of the desert. She imagined herself doing what self-help books often recommend, and she tried to give her anxieties and frustrations to God. Only it didn't work. No matter how earnestly she tried to give them to God, she imagined God giving them back to her. Her unnamed concerns took the form of a cross hopping down the road, trying to catch up with her, unwilling to be given away just yet. "Could it be that I'm not able to give this particular hopping cross up now because I have some learning to do?" she writes.

> If so, I must do my best to carry the thing as patiently as I can and figure out what it is I'm supposed to be doing in my soul-work. Could be that something needs to change— some circumstance I don't know about . . . before I can be at peace again?[11]

These experiences—of feeling that something is trying to get our attention—are common in desert times. And just as Troi and

> *Why do you stand so far off, O Lord,*
> *and hide yourself from me in time of trouble?*
>
> —PSALM 10:1 (THE BOOK OF COMMON PRAYER 1979)

Molly Wolf discovered, we usually experience them as something without a name, something that niggles at us but not in any clear and understandable way, at least not at first. It's easy to become like Chester Filbert and try to ignore them, to pretend that nothing's happening. "The signs that presage growth, so similar, it seems to me, to those in early adolescence: discontent, restlessness, doubt, despair, longing, are interpreted falsely as signs of decay . . . ," writes Anne Morrow Lindbergh in her book, *Gift from the Sea*.

> Because of a false assumption that it is a period of decline, one interprets these life-signs, paradoxically, as signs of approaching death. Instead of facing them, one runs away. . . . Anything, rather than stand still and learn from them. One tries to cure the signs of growth, to exorcise them, as if they were devils, when really they might be angels of annunciation.[12]

If these feelings are, indeed, angels of annunciation, times of transition invite us to befriend them and let them do their job. Let them deliver whatever message they came to reveal. In one of my favorite Christmas books, illustrator Julie Vivas pictures Gabriel swooping down on a startled young Mary, who is hanging the wet laundry on the line. On the next page, Gabriel and Mary sit together at the kitchen table with cups of tea in hand discussing Gabriel's annunciation. That's how I picture the time in the desert. We're invited to look behind and around us to see the cross hopping along, trying to catch up with us, or the vision in the night that won't let us go, or the angel swooping down on laundry day, and invite them in for a cup of tea. Rather than try to banish troublesome feelings—boredom, restlessness, fear, loneliness, anxiety, or whatever form the angels of annunciation take—invite them to dinner and listen to what they came to say. You can always say no to their invitation, just as Mary might have said no to Gabriel.

In Mercer Mayer's children's book *There's a Nightmare in My Closet*, a young boy hides under his covers and trembles each night because he knows there's a nightmare in his closet just waiting to get him. One night, tired of being frightened all the time, he summons his courage, grabs his toy sword, and flings open the door, exposing the huge monster. Only now the monster is the frightened one. Faced with the brave little boy, the monster begs the boy not to hurt him. The little boy befriends the monster—the angel of annunciation—that has frightened him all these years, and the two of them crawl into bed and go to sleep peacefully.

 Do not be afraid, stand firm, and see the deliverance that the Lord will accomplish for you today.

—Exodus 14:13

What remains hidden—unapproachable—is always more frightening before it is exposed to the light. Canaan, even with its riches, overwhelms us, and we're afraid to go on in. It's so easy to see only the giants, the difficulty ahead, and ignore the ripe fruits, the flowing milk and honey, as most of the Israelite spies did on their first approach to Canaan. Feelings of fear and anxiety, as well as boredom and frustration, lead most of us to want a golden calf—a new and visible god that will defeat whatever negatives exist in our lives at the moment. It's natural to want that. But it doesn't work.

The Israelites had a very difficult time learning to listen to these kinds of feelings. Or perhaps they listened but rather than engage them in conversation, they let the feelings completely over-whelm them. They weren't willing or able to listen for wisdom in their new situation. Most of the time they wanted to banish their anxieties, as Molly Wolf tried to do. They tried to take charge of things and knock God out of the process, or they blamed God for their liberation rather than take the time to notice what God was bringing about in their lives. "Why have you brought us out of Egypt to die in the wilderness?" (Numbers 21:5) they cried over and over again. And who can blame them? I've said the same thing to God many times in my life.

God is patient with them, up to a point, but God finally seems to have had enough of the people's accusations and rebel-liousness. In a troubling story from Numbers, God sends poison-ous snakes—very odd angels of annunciation—to bite and kill the people. Realizing that they've sinned once again, the people ask Moses' help, and Moses goes to God, who instructs him to make a serpent and set it on a pole. If people will look up at the bronze snake after a poisonous snake has bitten them, they will live. The poisonous snakes don't go away. Such angels rarely disappear com-pletely, any more than those unpleasant feelings do. But God tells the people to look up at the serpent of bronze on the pole. That's all they have to do. God asks them to look at the very thing that's killing them—a snake. In much the same way, God may be saying, "Look at what you're running away from." The snake that can kill you is an angel of annunciation, if you'll only befriend it.

What the Israelites needed to do in their time of restlessness, boredom, and fear was to help each other remember what God had done for them, to trust that God loved them and wasn't oblivi-ous to their pain. Instead they sat around remembering the "good life" they had in Egypt, whipping each other into a frenzy of anx-iety rather than trusting that God might be guiding them to some-thing new and glorious. They kept looking backward instead of forward, a topic I'll explore in the next chapter. They wanted to know if they "were there yet" but didn't even recognize "there"—Canaan—when they got to it the first time.

Transition time—desert time—is for just being and noticing what's taking shape. It's the long walk up the steep mountain in hopes that the view is worth the trouble. Or turning around to the cross that's hopping down the road behind you and asking it to state its name. It's being single for the first time in many years and wondering if you're going to be by yourself for the rest of your life or being retired after focusing only on work for fifty years and wondering what to do with the days ahead. The desert is a place to learn how to be with God in uneventful times. It's sitting in the desert, gathering manna daily, hanging out, and wondering what's next. And it's about noticing what *is* going on—about turning around and looking at the block you live on instead of sitting with your back to it.

Terry Waite, who went to Lebanon in 1987 to help negotiate the release of American captives, was captured himself and held in prison for several years, most of it in solitary confinement. Since his release, he has written and spoken about this period of his life, and he speaks of surviving the time in prison, in part, by writing his autobiography in his head. His captivity, difficult as it was—and with nothing to do; boredom and anxiety were his only companions—led him forward, as he recounts in "Footfalls in Memory":

Almighty God, who knowest our necessities before we ask, and our ignorance in asking: set free thy servants from all anxious thoughts for the morrow; give us contentment with thy good gifts; and confirm our faith that according as we seek thy kingdom, thou wilt not suffer us to lack any good thing; through Jesus Christ our Lord.

—St. Augustine

My captivity was certainly a miserable experience which I would not wish to go through again. And yet, almost despite myself, something had come from it. . . . I know I was able to take the experience of captivity and turn it into something creative. There was a cost, a high and painful cost, and at times the pain lingers. There have been benefits. I have learnt to embrace solitude as a friend and I no longer experience the aching loneliness which made me such a compulsive individual. I have long appreciated the beauty of form and order in life, but I no longer feel so insecure that I have to be dogmatic to the point of arrogance.[13]

Desert time invites us to befriend all that restlessness, boredom, anxiety, and fear or whatever other emotions you're experiencing. The down time in all transitions is the time we need for giving up what was and working with God to co-create what will be. It's the time to re-live the old stories, to reflect on what was, and then to begin looking ahead and dreaming about what's coming. Desert time is about letting go of your old name—the name you have been called by all of these years—and learning a new one, just as God gave Abram the name Abraham as he grew more fully into the person God hoped he would be.

This isn't a process of dying to the self; it is about becoming more of the self that God wishes into being. I remember hating the name I was known by as a child. The name Debbie never seemed to fit me. I tried to get friends and family to call me by my middle name, Kelli, but that didn't catch on with anyone. So for years I lived with a name that didn't feel like my own. In my early twenties I took a job that became, for me, the base of my professional career, a job that helped me learn about who I really was and what I was called to do in this life. In that job, managing a large book division, my staff members' names were Terry, Jerry, Larry, Gary, Debbie, and then me—another Debbie. That's when I became Debra and discovered the name that was truly mine. Becoming Debra—the name that had always been on my birth certificate—was a time of becoming more of myself, more of what God called me to be. It is most often in the desert, in transitional times, that we begin to discover our true name—and the dreams that go along with it.

In the midst of the desert, it's easy to ignore the dreams and hopes that begin to pop up unexpectedly. Sometimes we're so focused on our loss, like the Israelites, that the new emerging life gets short shrift.

- Keep track in your journal of dreams, hopes, desires—any angels of annunciation—that come to you in the desert.
- Write down anything that comes to you, without worrying about its practicality or about having to act on the dream. This is a time for dreaming, not acting.

In the middle of transitional time, it's so easy to pay attention to the negatives, to the loss or pain, as the Israelites did. Recording your dreams and hopes will help you focus on what may be emerging as new life, as God's desires for you as you move toward Canaan.

∿ The Blessing of Not Being "There" ∿

I've moved across the country a few times over the last decades, and usually I fly to my new home. But once I had the time to drive from California to my new home in New York. A friend accompanied me on that five-day journey, and we spent the time talking, listening to music, or just sitting in silence as the scenery went past. Perhaps in this day of quick flights from here to there, we've lost something valuable: time to make the transitions we need to make. On the drive from Berkeley to Syracuse, I had time to absorb the transition happening in my life. I drove out of town crying, aware of my sadness at leaving people and places I loved, for a situation that was largely unknown. I was also aware that after several weeks of saying goodbye to people, I was exhausted with farewells. As the distance between me and my old home increased, I experienced a lightening of the sorrow. My old life receded into the distance, both literally and figuratively, and my focus began to shift toward the future. There was something powerful and necessary about those five days of being neither here nor there yet. The time in the car between California and New York was definitely a blessing.

This kind of time in the transition process—time where we don't have to be who we were and when we don't have to know who we're going to be yet—usually seems less a gift than a nuisance in desert seasons, but few people make it through the desert without enduring some of this time. Like the Israelites, we find it hard to let go of being what we were—slaves, in the case of the Israelites—and live into a new way of being the beloved children of God. Most of us need—and must learn to live with—time when we're not "there" yet, challenging as that may be.

 When Pharaoh let the people go, God did not lead them by way of the land of the Philistines, although that was nearer. . . . God led the people by the roundabout way of the wilderness toward the Red Sea.

EXODUS 13:17–18

Having space—often physical space—to do that makes a difference in the quality of the journey. God gave the Israelites plenty of space to make their transition from being slaves to being the people of God. The desert stretched out before them for decades until they were ready to move into the land God promised them.

The natural world often models how clearing a space—sometimes in the form of something destructive—makes room for new life. On May 18, 1980, a volcanic eruption blew 1,300 feet off the top of Mount St. Helens in Oregon. The pictures of the area right after the devastation showed a bleak and barren landscape. Little was left except ash, debris, and charred remains. And yet the destruction wasn't complete; it never is. Various seeds and plant life, as well as some wildlife, survived the blast. Burrowing pocket gophers and insects began rebuilding. Bulbs and roots of various sorts began to collect and then grow in crevices created by the dried lava. Together they reshaped the mountaintop. Today Mount St. Helens, not the one of old but a new one, teams with wildlife, flowers, and new forest. The mixture is different from what existed. The destruction of the dense forest shade that prevented the growth of new life is gone, and smaller life forms have established themselves where that was impossible before. The blast that removed so much of the mountain and the life that used to exist has—over time—created space for new life.

People in the midst of transition can also find it helpful to make some space for themselves, to remove themselves from familiar settings, at least for a while. The couple whose children are all gone move to a smaller house. The widow redecorates or renovates the house she shared with her husband. The woman in the midst of a midlife crisis takes a week to go on retreat, away from all she knows so she can rest and simply be with God for a while. Being away from physical space that is associated with what was and who we were can be as critically important to us as it was for the Israelites in the desert.

Sometimes what we need isn't only physical space but emotional separation from aspects of our previous life, including people whom we've called friends, even people who love us. Too often friends and loved ones want to hurry us through transitional times.

After the first few months of my own diagnosis of MS, friends suggested that I write about living with illness. Other friends told me about writers who'd written about their life with MS, encouraging me to read and think about writing something like that. I might have done that, but I didn't have much to say at the time. I hadn't really gotten to know the illness very well yet, and I didn't know what I had to say. I suspect that the encouragement of friends was their way of trying to comfort me, to help me come to grips with the diagnosis, and I appreciated their concern on one level. I also recognized that their suggestions came from their own anxiety, rather than mine, and that I needed a break from their worry.

Recently, a famous ice skater got what seemed like the flu. Exhausted, he rested completely for two days. Two days of rest turned into a week, and the week into four weeks. Throughout that time he worried about how he was going to get back into shape for competitive skating, how he could re-train himself back to the high level he was used to. He is a singles skater (which means he skates solo, rather than with a partner), in his early thirties, which is on the older side for competitive singles skaters. As he listened to his body throughout the four weeks of enforced rest, he realized that he didn't want to push himself as hard as he'd need to in order to get back to skating competitions. He also realized there were parts of his life that he'd ignored or given short shrift to while he was skating competitively, that there were other things he wanted to do. So he's left the skating world, at least for now, and is exploring some of the other areas in his life that intrigue him. I wonder whether he would have been able to reflect and re-focus his life had he continued to be surrounded by the skating community—a community he probably cares deeply about.

What each person needs in transition will vary from what another needs. Sometimes a transition calls us to physically be still, as it did for the figure skater. Stopping, resting, and waiting are tasks on our to-do list. Sometimes what we most need and want to do is move—physically move elsewhere—even break ties with those we have loved. Other desert journeys allow for going on with the parts of our lives, even at moderate levels. If we can work and meet some or all of our obligations, and if those are still meaningful to us, that's great. If work isn't possible, as with the skater, and we can't handle all the responsibilities we had before the transition began, then that's reality for now. Maybe that will be reality for a long time. Still the time of waiting doesn't have to involve sitting on the curb, like Chester Filbert, with chin dragging.

> *I wait for the LORD,*
> *my soul waits, and in*
> *his word I hope;*
>
> *my soul waits for the*
> *Lord more than those*
> *who watch for the*
> *morning, more than*
> *those who watch for the*
> *morning.*
>
> —PSALM 130:5–6

The desert offers us the gift of time to slow down, to listen and pay attention to what's taking shape, to watch for whatever angels of annunciation lurk around us.

In the midst of your own transition, pay attention to whatever distracts you from the desert journey. Try to simply notice how you're spending your days and nights without judging yourself. Are you taking care of yourself—getting enough quiet time, sleep, rest, exercise, and so on— or do you find yourself filling your day with a to-do list? In a transition of my own, I found that I was unconsciously doing everything I could to avoid prayer and quiet time. I didn't really want to provide God with any opportunity to talk with me, probably because I didn't know what God would say and wasn't sure I wanted to hear it anyway. If your experiences are similar to mine, try some of the following:

- If you're finding that you're too busy, too tired, too frustrated in the midst of the desert, try making a list of the activities and tasks that occupy your days.

- Make some conscious decisions about whether all of these are things you want or need to do.
- Find some time—even just five minutes daily—to sit quietly with God and simply listen. Even if you don't hear anything or sense that anything's happening, trust that over time your willingness to be quiet and attentive to God will help you see what God is doing in your life and how you are being re-shaped.
- If you find it difficult to just be silent with God, consider beginning your prayer times with the following prayer:

Pilgrim God, there is an exodus going on in my life: desert stretches, a vast land of questions. Inside my head your promises tumble and turn. No pillar of cloud by day or fire by night that I can see. My heart hurts at leaving loved ones and so much of the security I have known. I try to give in to the stretching and the pain. It is hard, God, and I want to be settled, secure, safe and sure. And here I am feeling so full of pilgrim's fear and anxiety.

O God of the journey, lift me up, press me against your cheek. Let your great love hold me and create a deep trust in me. Then set me down, God of the journey; take my hand in yours, and guide me ever so gently across the new territory of my life.[14]

—JOYCE RUPP

CHAPTER VI

You Put Your Right Foot In, You Put Your Right Foot Out

My heart was wilderness
I heard your voice;
my grief divided me
you held me close;
bitterness consumed me
you overflowed with trust;
I longed to be with you
you let me stay.[1]

—JANET MORLEY

She was already sobbing when I got to my seat. A little girl, flying with her mother, was in tears. "I want my daddy," she kept insisting. Her mother tried to comfort her, but the only response she got was the same sentence: "I want my daddy." The minute the plane took off, the lament changed. "I want to go back!" she said over and over. Not until about half an hour into the flight did she stop sobbing and begin to play with the toys that her mom had brought with them. That lasted for a while. Then she'd take a break from the toys to lament again. Bouncing between the present (her toys) and what was behind her (her daddy, at least temporarily), she reminded me of a childhood game—the hokey-pokey. Everyone stands in a circle and sings, while doing the motions described in the song. "You put your right foot in/ You put your right foot out/ You put your right foot in and you shake it all about./ You do the hokey-pokey and you turn yourself around./ That's what it's all about." That's a pretty clear description of one phase of the transition process: the time when we have to make a decision about moving forward or living in the past. Rarely does anyone manage to move forward without taking a few steps backward first.

∿ I Want to Go Back! ∿

In the midst of the desert times, it's all too easy to count the losses and, like the little girl on the plane, to want to go back to what was. "Like Job," writes Roman Catholic spirituality writer Joyce Rupp in her book *Little Pieces of Light*, "we all long to have life return to the way it used to be, or the way we have longed for it to be."[2] Rupp's wise comment highlights the difficulty of this part of transitions. In the middle of uncomfortable and unfamiliar territory, it's tempting to put on rose-colored glasses and see a past that was better—or *even* better—than it actually was. Any past, whether it was rosy not, looks better than the continued discomfort of a strange and unknown future.

At the local minor-league ballpark where I live, the audience plays a game between the third and fourth innings that reminds me of the anxiety that surrounds the choices faced in transitions. A person in the stands gets to choose one of three gifts. One gift is specified; usually it's something okay but not extraordinary. The other two gifts are secret. One is in an envelope held by the announcer, and the other is in a truck on the baseball field. The choice, for the person selected to play, is between something known and two unknowns.

That's uncomfortably like the choice each of us faces in transition. What's ahead—in a sealed envelope or a truck out on the field—might or might not offer as much promise as a past we know. After all, how could anyone or anything replace that great love of our lives? Or the city in which we've lived for twenty years? That great job? Far too many emotions can kick in and overwhelm us as we contemplate the choices: fear of the unknown, the worry that we're betraying someone as we move on, fear of failure, the fear of making the wrong decision, and countless others. Sometimes it's easier to simply respond as the Israelites did and look backward at Egypt and slavery with a fondness that's based more on fiction than on fact.

At the edge of the promised land, after forty years of wandering in the desert, the Israelites finally got the chance to choose between the known—life in the desert or going back to Egypt—and the unknown—that land of milk and honey that God had been promising them for so long. God brought them to the edge of Canaan (Numbers 13) and gave them instructions for taking the land that God had promised them. But they feared what lay ahead. Taking the land from the people already there, not knowing whether the land was really

You desire truth in the inward being; therefore teach me wisdom in my secret heart.

PSALM 51:6

good or not, among other unknowns, were too much for most of them; they got to thinking about how "wonderful" life had been in Egypt and decided not to accept the gift of the land. Looking backward and creating rosy pictures of their lives as slaves and being honest about what had been was more comforting than facing the unknown.

Sometimes it looks easier—and safer—to look backward instead of forward. Adrienne Rich, a contemporary poet, tells the story of searching for what actually *was* (versus what was not) in her poem, "Diving into the Wreck." The journey she describes is a courageous one that is not to be undertaken lightly. She envisions herself climbing down a ladder from a boat into the sea and swimming down to the depths to discover not only the wreck that is there but, more importantly, the treasures.[3]

Uncovering the wreck—being real and truthful about what we're leaving behind, be it wonderful or difficult—that's some of the hardest work of transition. Fear of going down and seeing the real wreck can prevent us from seeing the treasures that may await us there. Looking honestly at the wreck, choosing not to mythologize whatever is behind us, is the only way to move forward into what God most hopes and desires for us. Being honest about what was and walking forward, even when we know what land we're being called to, is challenging. The Israelites weren't the only ones in history to look back in fondness on the life they knew for fear of moving forward; most of us have done or will do the same at some point in our lives.

∿ Chicken or Eagle? ∿

Walking in the woods one day, a man found an eagle's egg, apparently abandoned. He took it and placed it in the nest of one of his chickens, where it eventually hatched. The eaglet grew up as a chicken, scratching at the ground and digging for worms and bugs. He even learned to cluck like the other chickens. Every once in a while, he flapped his wings and flew a few feet into the air, but he never tried to fly any higher than that.

One day, he saw a splendid bird soaring gracefully above him over the landscape. "Who's that?" he asked the other chickens, who told him it was an eagle. "What a magnificent bird," the eagle thought to himself. "Too bad I'm a chicken." And so the eagle spent his entire life on the ground, living as a chicken, and died without ever realizing that he was, in fact, an eagle.[4]

The choice that the eagle avoided making is the same one the Israelites faced at the edge of Canaan, the same one most of us face at some point in the desert journey. Will we continue to be a chicken, which isn't what God most hopes for us, or will we find the courage to soar and be the eagle we're called to be? Put another way, how can we find the courage to listen to our heart's deepest desires and to listen for what God seems to hope for us and choose to walk forward into the unknown? How do we know we're actually an eagle and not a chicken?

 O send out your light and your truth; let them lead me; let them bring me to your holy hill and to your dwelling.

PSALM 43:3

There aren't any simple or concrete answers to these questions, and the challenges differ from person to person. For one person, letting go of what was proves to be the biggest barrier to moving forward. For another, it's the fear of the unknown that gets in the way. Yet another person finds herself afraid to embrace the dreams she has. At some point, however, we either have to refuse to move ahead and choose to stay where we are or move forward in hope and faith that this is, indeed, where we're supposed to be going right now. God beckons us to come forward, but the choice is always ours.

The well-known writer Madeleine L'Engle talks about that same kind of decision when she writes about the artist and her art-work. . . .

> The artist must be obedient to the work, whether it be a symphony, a painting, or a story for a small child. I believe that each work of art, whether it is a work of great genius or something very small, comes to the artist and says, "Here I am. Enflesh me. Give birth to me." And the artist either says, "My soul doth magnify the Lord," and willingly becomes the bearer of the work, or refuses. . . .[5]

Though L'Engle is talking about the process of creating art, her words also speak to the process of co-creating ourselves in the midst of transition. At some point in the desert journey, God comes to us as a still small voice, as an inkling of some sort, as intuition, and says, "Enflesh me. Give birth to me." And like a painter or writer or sculptor, we can either answer, "I will, with God's help," or we can refuse, as the Israelites did at the edge of Canaan.

∿ Letting Go ∿

Writer Margaret Silf tells the story of an old man who sensed that death was close and asked his children to take him out into his beloved yard, where he picked up a clump of the dirt on the land he loved so dearly. He'd lived on this land all his life, and he couldn't imagine not taking just a bit of it with him. He died just a short time later, still clutching the soil.

He arrived at the gateway to Heaven a little while later, where he was warmly greeted and welcomed, but only on the condition that he let go of the soil. He refused, so he had to remain outside the gate of Heaven for several years, until, once again, he was invited in. Still he refused to let go of the soil of his beloved land, so he was consigned to continue living outside Heaven. Many years later the angels came again to invite him in, but this time they brought his granddaughter—who had now died—with them. The man was so overjoyed to see his granddaughter that he dropped the soil as he raced over to embrace her, and they went into Heaven together.[6]

Entering into Canaan—moving on into new life—requires that we let go of the soil from a land where we don't live any longer, that we let go of what is now past. That process begins in the mourning stage for most people, but perhaps it has its completion at the stage in the journey when the choice to move forward presents itself. Letting go doesn't imply that we forget whatever or whomever we loved and never think of them again. It's more like what Jean Vanier, founder of the L'Arche communities in France and other countries that care for people with severe disabilities, describes when he talks about holding a wounded bird in his hand. Henri Nouwen, who spent a lot of time at the L'Arche community, repeats Vanier's explanation.

> He asks: "What will happen if I open my hand fully?" We say: "The bird will try to flutter its wings, and it will fall and die." Then he asks again: "But what will happen if I close my hand?" We say: "The bird will be crushed and die." Then he smiles and says: "An intimate place is

like my cupped hand, neither totally open nor totally closed."[7]

Letting go, at this point in the desert journey, is the process of holding what was—loved ones, important places, or situations—lightly, without having to release them entirely, but without holding them tightly either. The Celtic peoples were perhaps the masters of the art of loving and yet moving forward into the places God called them to go. For a period of over five hundred years, Celtic monks and others practiced *perigrinatio,* a word that Esther de Waal tells us translates to a combination of wandering exile and pilgrimage.[8] These *peregrinati,* or pilgrims, set off on foot or in small boats without oars, and they went wherever God called them to go. Some spent years at sea, letting the winds and waves take them where they would, believing that God guided their course the entire way. They set out on their journeys in great confidence and faith in God's guidance, but, as de Waal reminds us, they never stopped missing their homeland. "However intense the desire and however total the commitment to undertake this exile for the love of Christ, it remained extremely costly. They all retained this intense love and longing for their native homeland whenever they were away from it."[9] We too may choose to move on, even while feeling intense love for whatever or whomever we have to leave behind.

Like the child who has to give up his security blanket or his imaginary friend in order to move on, we have to learn to let go or at least hold far more lightly whatever keeps us living in the past. That isn't done overnight; the Israelites had trouble doing it in forty years. Learning to let go, and the reward for letting go, is illustrated by the story of the doll made of salt. As the doll wanders through life looking for answers to the question of who she is, she finally comes to the edge of the sea. "Who are you?" she asks the sea, and the sea invites her to come in and find out. She hesitates at first, but as she walks into the water and dissolves little by little, she discovers who she is. Times of transitions are like that. When we walk into the sea, what we have been—the sum of all our experiences—dissolves into something bigger and greater, something more like what God hopes for us.

Sometimes that experience sneaks up on us, and we don't recognize that Canaan is either in front of us or just a couple of miles ahead. In a workshop once, I asked the group assembled to make a list of the losses in their lives. After they had done that, I invited them to make a list of what they'd gained. As we debriefed each other after making the two lists, one of the participants, who had been quietly crying during the exercise, told all of us: "This is the first time that I've realized that my gains are more than my losses."

Sometimes we've been wrapped up for so long with what we've lost (as the Israelites were) that we forget to look forward. Hanging on to what we miss, looking backward for it, we don't always turn to see what's ahead. Doing that once in a while can help put life as it is today into perspective, so I encourage you to try the exercise I asked my group to do.

Helper of All Who Are Helpless,

we call on You

in times of stress

and in times of devastation.

Pick up the broken pieces

of our hearts, our homes, our history

and restore them to the way they were

or give us the means of starting over

when everything seems lost.

O God, Our Help in Ages Past,

we place all our hope in You.

Amen.[10]

—MIRIAM THERESE WINTER

Spend some quiet time making a list of what you've lost, and then do the same with what you've gained. Write down everything you can think of on both lists, censoring yourself as little as possible. No one else needs to see the lists. You can do this all in one sitting if you wish, or just keep a list going in your journal and record everything that comes to mind over the course of a few days or weeks. When the lists feel complete, ask yourself:

- What do you notice about the two lists? Does anything you wrote surprise or challenge or comfort you?
- What emotions did you experience as you were writing the lists? Were the emotions the same or different as you worked on the two lists?
- Is there any discernable invitation from God that you can find in the list of gains?
- If so, does that give you any additional courage for moving forward?

∿ Dealing with the Great What-Ifs ∿

All transitions involve walking through a door that prevents our seeing what's ahead. A new city to live in, a new school or job, life as a newly single person or a newly sober person, and all other transitions involve dealing with something unknown that's going to stretch us. The unknown is a scary place, even when it comes with some sense of excitement. It's not unusual for the imagination to begin to work overtime and for the great what-ifs to set in. What if the new employer doesn't like my work? What if I can't figure out how to balance the checkbook without my husband's help? What if I can't find another job? What if nobody likes me sober? Many of us can "what-if" ourselves until we're almost paralyzed with fear or anxiety.

The Israelites let the great what-ifs get the best of them at the edge of Canaan. The first thing the spies told Moses, on returning from their look at Canaan, was that the land flowed with milk and honey and produced good fruit. "But . . ." they quickly added. (We've always got a "but" to add!) But there were strong people who would defeat the Israelites. Caleb, one of the spies, calmed everyone: the land is good and the people can be overcome with God's help. But the older spies continued to worry, to let the what-ifs get the best of them. Now the strong people became giants, who would just step on the Israelites as if they were grasshoppers. In the end, the Israelites allowed themselves to be swayed by the spies' exaggerated stories. Their fears about all the bad things that might happen overwhelmed the promises that God had been making to them for decades in the desert. Their fears—the what-ifs—overwhelmed their own lived experience that God provided what they most needed, over and over again. And so God sent them back to the desert to wander some more. The people were not ready to move forward.

The fear the Israelites felt at the edge of their new life is the same one many people feel as they contemplate moving forward.

> *Remember your word to your servant, in which you have made me hope.*
>
> *This is my comfort in my distress, that your promise gives me life.*
>
> —PSALM 119:49–50

Most of us enjoy learning something new once in a while. We like an occasional and manageable challenge. But transitions call us toward something more major, something deeper than learning to create a new kind of report on the computer or to cook a soufflé. More often than not, they call us to live differently, sometimes very differently. It takes a lot of courage to summon up the strength to quell those fears and walk over the border into the new land.

Two pieces of snow-white paper faced that challenge once. They were most proud of their pure and dazzling whiteness, which formed the core of their self-identity. One day a painter with brushes and paints in hand walked down the road toward them. In panic they began to imagine what the man could possibly want with them and realized that, in all likelihood, he wanted to paint them. With horror the first piece of white paper ran away, unwilling to allow the painter to put his vision on her. The second piece of paper was a bit braver and let the painter approach. "May I paint you?" the painter asked her. (The painter, like God, always asks whether we are willing to cooperate.) The paper gave her assent, and the painter created a painting on her that many admired for years afterward.[11]

The story of the two pieces of paper raises an interesting dilemma. As we look at the what-ifs, how do we know whether we're just being anxious, like Moses at the burning bush (or the first piece of paper), or whether the challenges are genuinely insurmountable or unacceptable? That's worth sorting out as you stand at the edge of Canaan.

"It is helpful to remember," writes Joyce Rupp, "that most fears are never realized. They rarely actually happen. They are bullying Goliaths, pushing the little David in us around, trying to paralyze us with inaction so that we do not grow into the person we are meant to be."[12] With God's help, we can release our fears and move forward, growing into the person God hopes we will become.

One way to dispel fears is to envision the worst-case scenario. What is the most awful thing that could happen as a result of moving forward? Occasionally—and only occasionally—the consequences are potentially serious or even fatal. On the evening news one night, I heard the story of two people who had served their military time in a war zone and been sent home. Both went back to the war zone as civilians to help in the rebuilding effort because they felt called to help the people, despite the volatile nature of the region. Terrorist bombs killed them as they tried to help the people rebuild their lives. But each of them knew the danger they faced and nevertheless chose to return. If the worst-case scenario involves danger at this level, even if it seems God is calling you to take that step forward, ask yourself if you are truly able and ready to move forward. We have a choice. Like the two soldiers who return as rebuilders, the answer may be yes. If the answer is no, my experience is that God understands this and will invite us to move forward again when we're ready, just as God brought the Israelites back to Canaan when they were ready.

The what-ifs have their place in transition, but they can tempt us away from trusting God's guidance if we entertain them for too long or come to understand them as absolute truth. I came to that place of trust as I learned to give myself shots and do what I can to live well with multiple sclerosis. I've talked to many people who've lived with the disease for a long time and read the magazine stories about what might lie ahead for me. I've also talked to some extraordinary people who have MS who, despite challenging physical problems, live rich lives filled with God's grace and presence. I know what *could* happen to me; I don't know what *will* happen to me. But I am convinced that God will give me

To you, O LORD, I lift up my soul.

O my God, in you I trust; do not let me be put to shame; do not let my enemies exult over me.

Do not let those who wait for you be put to shame; let them be ashamed who are wantonly treacherous.

Make me to know your ways, O LORD; teach me your paths.

Lead me in your truth, and teach me, for you are the God of my salvation; for you I wait all day long.

Be mindful of your mercy, O LORD, and of your steadfast love, for they have been from of old.

—PSALM 25:1–6

the resources to deal with whatever I must deal with in the future, just as God has given me what I've needed throughout the rest of my life. The what-ifs still hang out there, floating around for me to latch onto if I let them. Some days I do succumb. Some days I'm convinced that I have a new symptom that indicates a worsening of the disease. Or I go through one of my periods of disequilibrium and fatigue, and I'm convinced that I'm never going to get through all I feel I have to do. But without being a Pollyanna about the whole thing, for the most part, I'm keeping the what-ifs at arm's length. When and if one of them becomes real, I'm sure that will be a struggle for me. I'll have another season in the desert to contend with. I also know that I'll find Canaan again, with God's help.

Take some time to make a list of the what-ifs that threaten to paralyze you. Take your time making the list, and write down everything that frightens you, even if you think it sounds silly. Then consider the following questions. Journal about these if you find that helpful.

- What's the worst thing that could happen?
- Which, if any, of the what-ifs seem likely?
- Can you live with the consequences of a what-if becoming real?
- What part can or does God play in all of this for you?
- Has making this list and considering the possibilities lessened your anxiety about moving forward? Why or why not?
- Conclude your time of meditation or journaling with the following prayer:

God of strength, who calls forth eagles to bend wings in adoration, who sends forth eagles to bend wings to wing wide in praise, I am in need of your strength. I am weary,

tired, unable to soar in my sky of life. Carry me on your
loving wings. Renew my strength. Give me the energy for
the going and create in me an openness to future flying.
Great God of eagles' hearts, I want to trust that you will
bear me up, that you will support me. I look to you to
renew my strength just as surely as eagles' wings are wide
in the sky. Amen.[13]

—JOYCE RUPP

∿ Imaging the Mighty Might-Be's ∿

Brother Bruno was trying to pray one evening when a bullfrog disturbed his prayers. No matter how hard he tried to ignore the loud frog, he found himself distracted and unable to concentrate. Finally, in frustration he shouted at the frog to stop singing, which it did. Silence filled Brother Bruno's room, and he returned to his prayers. But an inner voice began to surface—one that wouldn't let him alone. "What if God is as pleased with the croaking of that frog as God is with your prayers?" the voice kept asking. And no matter how hard he tried, Brother Bruno couldn't let go of that thought. Finally, in utter frustration, he leaned out the window again and ordered the frog to sing. The bullfrog, along with all the other frogs in the area, began singing at once, and the sound of their croaking filled the air, making a harmonious and melodious sound. Brother Bruno listened to the sound with great delight and was finally able to focus on his prayers.[14]

Sometimes in the midst of transitions, we, like Brother Bruno, focus so much on what distresses us, on the what-ifs and the fear of moving forward, that we forget to listen for the possibilities that disturbances may offer. The what-ifs take center stage, and the wonderful things that "might be" sit in the wings, waiting to be noticed. And by and large, those might-be's are a lot more polite and quiet than the what-ifs. The what-ifs are bold and assertive, whereas the might-be's tend to be shy and hang back. They wait for us to approach them. Like the frog who was silent when Brother Bruno commanded it to be, the might-be's are unimposing. Like Brother Bruno, we have to let the frogs go ahead and sing if we're going to discover what God has in mind for us.

Caleb and Joshua were full of the might-be's on the edge of the land God had promised them. While all the spies' stories grew more exaggerated, more full of danger, risk, and certain death, Caleb and Joshua remained faithful to God and saw what might be in Canaan, instead of succumbing to the what-ifs. "The land that we went through as spies is an exceedingly good land," they tell the people (Numbers 14:7). God will bring them to the land of milk and honey, says Caleb. As in the time-worn cliché, he sees the glass as half-full.

To believe that the might-be's are possible is fundamentally an act of hope, and to be open to hope is to be vulnerable and at risk. It can also be just plain hard work sometimes, especially when the might-be's and the what-ifs look a lot alike, just as the wheat and the weeds did in a parable Jesus told.

> [Jesus] put before them another parable: The kingdom of heaven may be compared to someone who sowed good seed in his field; but while everybody was asleep, an enemy came and sowed weeds among the wheat, and then went away. So when the plants came up and bore grain, then the weeds appeared as well. And the slaves of the householder came and said to him, "Master, did you not sow good seed in your field? Where, then, did these weeds come from?" He answered, "An enemy has done this." The slaves said to him, "Then do you want us to go and gather them?" But he replied, "No; for in gathering the weeds you would uproot

the wheat along with them. Let both of them grow together
until the harvest" (Matthew 13: 24–30).

The difficulty in separating the wheat from the weeds is
another good reason to keep a journal of your hopes, dreams, and
desires throughout the transition process. It's a way of separating
the wheat and weeds over time. We sometimes have to be able to
live in the same space with both the what-ifs and the might-be's in
the middle of the desert and wait until harvest time—until we are
at the edge of Canaan—to tell the difference. Both the what-ifs
and the might-be's may have something to tell us.

To believe that the desert journey, with its conflicting emotions, promises, and threats, is not the space we'll live in forever, to
believe that there is something—a land of promise—ahead and
that God is calling us there requires courage. It requires the same
kind of courage that God asked of the Israelites at the edge
of Canaan. The first time they got there, they were too afraid to
trust that something wonderful
awaited them; only Caleb and
Joshua, as younger members of
the group who weren't attached
to Egypt, could dream about
what Canaan might be for them.
They were willing to think about
the might-be's instead of focusing
on the what-ifs. But the people as
a whole weren't ready to do that.
Not yet. They wandered in the
desert for many more years until
God brought the people back to
Canaan again. God extends the same invitation to us over and over
again, waiting for us to be ready to trust that whatever awaits us is
good and to find the courage to risk walking forward. God is

 *Open wide the window
of our spirits, O Lord,
and fill us full of light;
open wide the door of
our hearts, that we may
receive and entertain
you with all our powers
of adoration and praise.*

—CHRISTINA ROSSETTI

patient and will wait with us as long as need be, inviting us, the whole time, to imagine the might-be's until we can finally separate them from the what-ifs and enter the new life.

We each reach the place where we can begin to consider what might be ahead, and even get excited about the possibilities, in our own time. Some may be ready to look ahead after just a few months; others won't be ready to move on for years. The desert journey will be longer for some than it is for others; there are no set timetables in this kind of journey. But as remote as it may seem, there will come a time when you are ready to consider the future.

When you find yourself at a place where you might be willing to consider what possibilities lie ahead, try making a list of the might-be's, just as you made the list of what-ifs. Take some time to meditate quietly or journal on the following questions. It may take more than one session to adequately consider them; you may even find it helpful to let these questions rattle around in your head and heart for days or weeks.

- What's the best thing that could happen as you move forward?
- Which, if any, of the might-be's seem likely?
- Can you live with the consequences of a might-be becoming real?
- What part can or does God play in all of this for you?
- Has making this list and considering the possibilities lessened your anxiety about moving forward? Why or why not?
- Conclude your times of meditation or journaling with the following prayer:

Lord and Source of All Gifts,

we rejoice in the fullness of Your holy generosity.

We thank You especially now

for the gift of change

that gift of newness

that opens doors closed by habit and routine.

We thank You, O End of All Longing,

for the capacity for change in our lives,

for without change

there can be no real growth

and no true life.

Blessed be You, Lord our God,

who gives spice to life with change.[15]

—EDWARD HAYES

For most people the what-ifs and the might-be's alternate with each other. One morning the what-ifs win; the next day, the might-be's have the upper hand. The line from Egypt to Canaan isn't a straight or short one. Transitions, like the hokey-pokey, are about putting your foot in, taking it out, and doing that some more. In and out, back and forth—as the hokey-pokey song says: that's what it's all about.

CHAPTER VII

Home Again

*May the Lord keep our going out and our coming in
from this time on and for evermore.*
—Psalm 121:8

During a period of transition in her life, author Sue Monk Kidd kept a cocoon in her study, where it could remind her of her own process of trying to give birth to something she couldn't completely name. One morning when she awoke early and went to her study, she suddenly became aware that something was different. Looking around the room, she discovered that the chrysalis had opened and from it had emerged a beautiful butterfly. Kidd moved the pot in which the butterfly still perched out to the patio in order to let it fly free. It hesitated for a little bit, as if to get its bearings, and then finally flew away. Kidd writes:

> She had been with me such a long time, curled in her cocoon. . . . I'd watched over her. I'd loved her. Through her, God had watched over me, loved me, and taught me about the beauty and transformation of the soul. Now she flew. . . . When the time is right, the cocooned soul begins to emerge. Waiting turns golden. Newness unfurls. It's a time of pure, unmitigated wonder. Yet as we enter the passage of emergence, we need to remember that new life comes slowly, awkwardly, on wobbly wings.[1]

God makes a way in the desert for us in times of transition, and then one day, perhaps when we're not even expecting it, we awake and discover that the landscape has changed. Canaan, the goal of the journey, stands before us, and we are home—except that it's a new home, certainly not the one we knew, often not the one we expected.

And in many ways, standing at the edge of Canaan is when the journey begins all over again. Kidd describes watching the new butterfly sit on the branch of a plant for quite a while, readying itself for flight and new life. The time in the cocoon, like the time wandering in the desert, turns out to be preparation—a time to collect the resources needed to journey into new life. But this journey differs from the one in the desert because now there's a home base. There's a new life to adjust to, with new rules, new conditions, new challenges, new delights. There's still a journey to take, but we don't have to wander without knowing where we're headed. It's more akin to learning your way around a new city, but with a road map in hand.

The ending of one phase and the beginning of another can be hard to distinguish; the truth is that we spend much more of our lives in transition than out of it. Sometimes there's no real transition from the end of the desert to the beginning of the time in Canaan; one flows smoothly into the other, and only in retrospect is the difference between the two clear. Other changes are well defined, with endings that can be named. The recovering alcoholic is sober for sixty days and marks the occasion. The long-awaited divorce is final, and there's no going back. The papers for the new home have been signed. The couple is married. The child is born. But whether or not the transition point is marked, there comes a time for most of us when we arrive "there," and "there"—finally!—has a name. God has brought us safely to the place promised to us, and something in our hearts knows this is the place we're supposed to be. God, who blessed our going into the desert, now blesses our coming out of it.

 Lord, I am a countryman coming from my country to yours. Teach me the laws of your country, its way of life and its spirit, so that I may feel at home here.

—WILLIAM OF
ST. THIERRY

∿ Saying Goodbye ∿

Two monks were traveling from their home monastery to another one day, when they came to the edge of a river. A woman stood there; she wanted to get across but wasn't able to do it by herself. "Sit on my shoulders," the first monk told her, "and I'll carry you across." The woman gratefully accepted the offer and rode on the shoulders of the first monk, as they all crossed the river. On the other side the woman went her way, and the two monks went theirs.

As the two monks walked on in silence, the second monk—the one who hadn't carried the woman—made quiet huffing and snorting noises. The first monk realized that something was bothering his traveling companion. "What's bothering you, Brother?" he asked the second monk.

"You know we're forbidden to have any contact with women," the second monk replied. "Why did you carry that woman across the river?"

The first monk considered the criticism for a few minutes in silence. "I put that woman down at the other side of the river bank, Brother," he said. "Why are you still carrying her?"

There comes a time in transitions, usually after we have come to a new place that feels like home to us, that we need to put down the load we've been carrying, just as the first monk put down and parted company with the woman. Continuing to carry the emotions that were natural and appropriate companions on the desert journey is no more helpful to us than it was to the second monk who couldn't stop "carrying the woman" after he crossed the river. Once you've arrived, it's time to say goodbye to whatever is now in the past in a way that may not have been possible before.

When I moved to my new house recently, I put the condominium I'd been living in up for sale. I'd lived in the condo for about five years, and there were many aspects of living there that I loved. The space itself suited me wonderfully; I enjoyed the amount of light it got each day and the privacy I had. It was an easy place to maintain for someone like me who travels a lot. When the condo sold, I did my final cleaning in preparation for the new owner, and when it was all done I spent about an hour saying goodbye to the place that had been my home. I walked from room to room and remembered activities that had taken place in each. I thanked each room for its service, for protecting me from the elements, for making me feel welcome, for sharing life with me for five years. That was a sad afternoon for me; I cried as I walked from room to room. But it was a sweet sadness, filled with gratitude for all that had been rather than the sadness of regret. As I left the condo for what I knew would be the last time, it seemed as if I had done the final thing that needed to be done so that I could live in my new home without regret, and the new owner would have a home that was welcoming.

May the God of our past, our present and our future be with you today as you make a new beginning. May God heal the wounds caused by your incomplete attempts at loving, and strengthen your resolve to live in communion. May God look with mercy on the divisions in our larger world and lead us all to greater understanding. May your movement toward reconciliation contribute to a universe of peace and love. Amen.[2]

—KATHLEEN FISCHER
AND THOMAS HART

The goodbyes we say on entering into new life don't involve forgetting what once was or ceasing to love someone who was important. Far from it. These farewells, like my leave-taking at the condominium, are bittersweet. They're the honest expression of whatever feelings tether us to the past. They are ways of finally letting go of whatever prevents us from moving into the place God promises to us. This kind of farewell, when done honestly, allows us to look back at Egypt, recognize it for what it was, and then turn forward and walk into Canaan, ready for new life.

Sometimes those goodbyes involve expressing gratitude. The spouse who lost a beloved partner says farewell with a sense of deep thankfulness for their life together. Others say goodbye with regret: a divorce between two people who like each other still but who no longer love each other can be like this. Other times, saying farewell involves forgiving someone, or ourselves, for whatever has passed. Someone has hurt us or we have harmed someone else, but the time comes when forgiveness has to happen so both people can move on. Some farewells can be done in person; others are too painful or dangerous to do in person. There are also times when the people involved are no longer available to us, and the farewell has to be done another way. Whatever the circumstances, it's important to find a way to say the final things that need to be said. Hanging on to what has been only prevents us from entering Canaan and from growing more deeply into God's hopes and desires for us.

> *God our Lover and Friend, we give thanks for this person whose love has so enriched our life. Help us to carry his/her blessings as we say goodbye and move on. May he/she be an ongoing source of strength and joy.*[3]
>
> —KATHLEEN FISCHER
> AND THOMAS HART

If you're not sure how to say farewell, consider some of the suggestions in the sections that follow.

∾ Speaking the Words ∾

When possible, say what needs to be said aloud. You may be able to say goodbye to the person, to talk with him or her about some of your journey and why you're moving on. If you can't or don't want to do that in person, you can still say the words out loud.

Whether you're doing this in person or by yourself, prepare ahead of time. Think about what you most need to say. If it's helpful, make some notes about that for yourself, or write a letter to the person or situation you're leaving. This part of the process is very important; it allows you the time and space to focus on the farewell that needs to happen, as well as your feelings about leaving. If you plan to say goodbye in person, you may also find it helpful to consider what the other person might say so you're prepared for that.

If you wish to say goodbye in person, set a time and place to do that. As you enter into the conversation, remember that God's caring presence surrounds *both* of you, giving each of you the resources you need at that moment. Say what you need to say, and let the other person or situation respond. If this is truly the time for saying goodbye, you'll be able to hear what the other person needs to say without feeling that you must change his or her mind.

Risen Christ, enable us to shed the weight of these memories and give up clinging to a past we cannot change. Reach into our lives and give us freedom to embrace our limitations and let go of regrets. You who are our hope from generation to generation, we offer our hearts and the sorrow within them. Mend our brokenness and bless our connections.[4]

—KATHLEEN FISCHER
AND THOMAS HART

If you can't or don't want to have the conversation in person, find a quiet space where you can be alone for a while and pretend that the person you need to address is present. You may find it helpful to remember that whether you do this in person or not, God is present with you and with the one you're addressing, holding both of you close. Say what needs to be said, and spend some time in silence listening for whatever response the other person (or God) might make. Close your time of farewell with a prayer or some other expression of your gratitude for the opportunity to say goodbye.

◡ Writing a Letter ◡

I find that writing a letter that expresses my feelings is enormously helpful at times. Try it if you can't or don't want to say goodbye in person, or possibly do it in preparation for a conversation. Don't worry about writing well or correcting your spelling or any of the details. (Your ninth-grade English teacher isn't looking!) Just write without censoring or correcting yourself. Consider this, at least for now, a letter that you're not going to send, so say whatever needs to be said. If possible find a place to write where you can be by yourself, and let yourself feel whatever emotions are in your heart and soul while you're writing.

Writing letters can be particularly helpful when you need to talk to someone who isn't available, such as a deceased person, or to something that isn't even a person. You could, for instance, write a letter to an addiction that held you hostage in the past.

If the letter is one you don't want to mail or e-mail, find another way to send it on its way. There is something very powerful about writing what you need to write and then making sure that it goes away from you. Symbolically at least, you are delivering the letter, so you no longer need to think about the farewell.

Bury it in the yard or elsewhere; tear it into little pieces and release it, or perhaps burn it in the fireplace. If the letter turns out to be one you can and wish to send, put it aside for a couple of days to make sure that you're aren't sending something you'll later wish you hadn't. But if it's still something you want to mail, trust your instincts.

∿ Praying Your Farewell ∿

Sometimes goodbyes happen as spontaneous prayers that arise in a moment of insight. Catholic spirituality writer Joyce Rupp recounts such a moment in her book, *Praying Our Goodbyes*. Still feeling raw from the death of a good friend, she writes that she heard the sound of geese migrating for the season. The image of the geese going where they were supposed to helped her know that her friend, too, had gone where she needed to go. Rupp spoke to God in her heart at that moment and released her friend into God's care.[5]

As you look for or happen upon moments and ways to say goodbye, think of praying your goodbye as a conversation with God, nothing more difficult than a conversation or connection you have with friends. At a moment that seems appropriate, or at the time when an insight hits you, take a moment to tell God that you're releasing whatever is past into God's care. Tell God the same things you might have said to a person or situation: express your thanks for what was good; offer or accept forgiveness for any pain inflicted; speak whatever regrets you feel. Then imagine physically handing whatever you need to leave behind directly into God's hands. If that particular image is problematic or lacks meaning for you, feel free to find another image that helps you hand over your concerns to God's care.

∿ Embodying Your Farewell ∿

There is something particularly powerful about performing an action that expresses what the heart and soul are experiencing. Physical actions can reflect the emotional and spiritual significance of an event or place, and have a way of making the farewell more real. That's why attending the burial or scattering the ashes of a loved one who has died is so powerful. At times physical actions can even help us understand feelings that aren't entirely clear to us at an intellectual level.

In his book on pilgrimage, Franciscan priest Murray Bodo describes one man's annual ritual on the anniversary of his wife's death. He goes to her grave, with friends who knew her, and they pour gin on it, since his wife loved martinis.[6] Together the man and his friends remembered the life of the woman who died, as they told stories, prayed together, and poured the gin on her grave—a simple but powerful celebration of a life and relationships that were important.

You don't need to develop a complicated ritual or enactment for a farewell to have meaning. Religious services for important transitional moments have been developed and printed in various denominational prayer books that you can use if you like. But you can also either design your own simple ritual or just pay attention to an idea or desire that comes to you and respond to that. Walking through the rooms of my condominium, saying goodbye to each room, is an example of a simple ritual. Packing up the clothes of a loved one who has died and giving them away can be a powerful ritual. The packing and the sorting allow time for remembering, for expressing gratitude, for tears, and for farewells. Walking through the rooms of a home or a workplace that you're leaving, visiting the grave of a loved one, packing up reminders of what's past, and other actions of this sort can help you say goodbye. Find an activity that seems to say what you want to say. Invite

God to be a part of whatever action you take, knowing that God will help you bear both your joy and sorrow.[7]

∿ Saying Hello ∿

I closed on the mortgage for my new house on a Wednesday morning. I'd taken the day off from work so I could go spend some time there before moving in a few days later. I went to my condominium, got my two cats and a few basic supplies—a sleeping bag, toilet paper, some food—and went to the new house to spend some time there before anything much was added. I wanted to find out what the house was like before I started putting my own stamp on it.

I brought with me a basket of pansies to greet the new house, sort of a housewarming present from me to the space itself. (I was amused, a month later, to find that a mother rabbit was using the pansies I had planted in the front yard to disguise the opening of her hole, which held three baby bunnies. The pansies seemed to be a multipurpose, cross-species housewarming gift.) I spent the next two days and nights at the new house with only a few provisions. I did some cleaning, but mostly I just hung out and learned what the rooms looked like, where the sun shone at what time of day, what it felt like to be in the house at night. A friend came to dinner that first evening, and we had a picnic on the floor. I wandered in my new garden—it was early spring—and made guesses about what kinds of flowers might come up. I introduced myself to the fish that lived in the pond out back. I spent some time in prayer in the room that felt like the sacred space in the house. By the time the movers came a couple of days later, I felt as though the house had given me permission to move in, that it welcomed my presence.

In Western culture today, we don't usually do things like this to acknowledge new beginnings. We tend to just turn into the creator again and move right into whatever is new without taking the time to introduce ourselves or to get to know what's in the land we were promised. We sometimes forget that this is new ground, that though we may have been called or invited to this new place, it is just that—a new place, one full of things we haven't yet met and may not understand immediately. That makes this new "home" both exciting and just a little bit dangerous.

Those first nights in my new house were full of noises I didn't recognize, smells that were new to me. I got up to use the restroom in the middle of the night and was completely disoriented in the dark. None of my furniture had been moved in; nearly everything felt unfamiliar. And yet this was the house that seemed to have picked me. I watched it sit on the market for three months before deciding that I was supposed to live there. I wasn't looking for a new house, but I couldn't help feeling that it was looking for me. Even in its unfamiliarity, I knew it was Home.

Discovering that you are—finally—out of the desert and in a new place may be obvious. The discovery can have a definitive starting point, like when you move to a new home, city, or job. The Israelites knew that they'd entered Canaan. We know when we're moving, starting a new job, or welcoming a new life into the household.

Grant us, O God, your protection; and in your protection, strength; and in strength, understanding; and in understanding, knowledge; and in knowledge, the knowledge of justice; and in the knowledge of justice, the love of justice; and in that love, the love of existence; and in the love of existence, the love of God, God and all goodness. Amen.

—Ancient Welsh Prayer, source unknown

Other times, realizing that we're finally at the new place creeps up on us. Someone who has lived through a period of mourning may realize suddenly that life doesn't feel like life in the desert anymore, and hasn't for a little while. The young man who moves to a new city realizes after a while that the new place finally feels like home to him. The realization can hit in many ways. One day we just discover that we're at home in a way that we haven't been for a long time. The way ahead doesn't look like a long, empty road anymore, and Egypt no longer tugs at the heartstrings.

Whenever you realize that you are at home again—whatever home turns out to be for you—that is the time to mark that life is starting over again in some significant way, as I did with the picnic dinner in my new home the first night.

Being at home is also the place where we most powerfully recognize that God is and has always been present, both throughout the journey and at the new beginning. "Where can I go then from your Spirit?" asks the Psalmist.

> *Where can I flee from your presence?*
> *If I climb up to Heaven, you are there;*
> *if I make the grave my bed, you are there also.*
> *If I take the wings of the morning*
> *and dwell in the uttermost parts of the sea,*
> *Even there your hand will lead me*
> *and your right hand hold me fast.*
> *If I say, "Surely the darkness will cover me,*
> *and the light around me turns to night,"*
> *Darkness is not dark to you;*
> *the night is as bright as the day;*
> *darkness and light to you are both alike.*
> —Psalm 139:6–11

God has been with us all along, through restlessness, thirst, hunger, and doubt in the desert, just as the Holy One is here with us in the new place we can call Home. As was true for Miriam and Moses, who praised God and danced with the people to celebrate the safe passage of the Israelites through the Red Sea, now is a time for praise and thanksgiving. Moses' song of praise on the far side of the sea rings true for many on arriving home:

> Who is like you, O LORD, among the gods? Who is like you, majestic in holiness, awesome in splendor, doing wonders? You stretched out your right hand, the earth swallowed them. In your steadfast love you led the people whom you redeemed; you guided them by your strength to your holy abode. You brought them in and planted them on the mountain of your own possession, the place, O LORD, that you made your abode, the sanctuary, O LORD, that your hands have established. The LORD will reign forever and ever (Exodus 15:11–13, 17–18).

In my own tradition, the Easter Vigil, which occurs Saturday night before Easter morning, most closely resembles the part of the transition journey that is the approach and acknowledgment of being home again. The priest may offer these words during the service: "Through the Pascal mystery, dear friends, we are buried with Christ by Baptism into his death, and raised with him to newness of life. I call upon you, therefore, now that our Lenten observance is ended, to renew the solemn promises and vows of Holy Baptism, by which we once renounced Satan and all his works, and promised to serve God faithfully in his holy Catholic Church."[8]

The reaffirmation of our baptismal vows follows: Do you reaffirm your renunciation of evil and renew your commitment to Jesus Christ? Do you believe in God, Jesus Christ, and God the Holy Spirit? Will you continue in the apostle's teaching and fellowship, in the breaking of the bread, and in the prayers? Will you persevere in resisting evil, and whenever you fall into sin, repent, and return to the Lord? Will you proclaim by word and example the Good News of God in Christ? Will you seek and serve Christ in all persons, loving your neighbor as yourself? Will you strive for justice and peace among all people, and respect the dignity of every human being?

The answer to the first questions about belief is, "I do." But the answer to the rest of the questions is, "I will." Once we are in Canaan, it is time to turn our focus from ourselves and what we need and turn it outward toward a needy world. "I will," we say. "I will seek and serve, strive, respect, and proclaim." The desert journey is over, and it is time to acknowledge God who brought us through the desert safely and to reaffirm our faith and our willingness to act on that faith.

Eternal God, heavenly Father . . . Send us now into the world in peace, and grant us strength and courage to love and serve you with gladness and singleness of heart; through Christ our Lord. Amen.

—THE BOOK OF COMMON PRAYER 1979

The desert journey turns out to be one that is not, finally, about us. Or not completely about each one of us. It is a journey that, if we let it, calls us to be more fully who we are as part of the people of God. The end of the journey turns out not only to be about personal transformation but about enlarging our hearts so that God can dwell more fully there. Margaret Silf repeats the story of a man who answers a knock on his door one day. God greets him and says that he is looking for a home for his son. The man thinks about it and says that he could rent God a room. God wants to buy the whole house but settles for the room. As time goes on, the man rents God more and more room, but never the whole house. The man is worried about having some space left for himself, but God is patient and knows that, eventually, the man will give over his whole home.[9] God waits for each of us in much the same way. And each transition we go through, if we're attentive and willing to let the Divine One walk with us, brings God into another room in our hearts and souls, until God finally occupies the entire place.

This is also a time for being gentle with ourselves. Newness, as Sue Monk Kidd reminds us, unfurls slowly, and that means we're going to fly with wobbly wings for a while. A friend of mine is fond of reminding me, in moments of high stress or crisis, that this isn't a time for playing with chainsaws. What she means is that when we're surprised, in shock, or otherwise distracted, we should take care to avoid dangerous situations, like driving or playing with chainsaws (something I wouldn't do even if I weren't stressed!). The same is true in exploring the new place we find ourselves in. Like Kidd's butterfly, we may need to sit on the plant for a while, flap our wings a bit, and get a sense of the landscape and our abilities before launching out into the air.

"Getting a sense of the landscape" usually means continuing to take care of ourselves, just as was true in the desert. The new home may be exciting, but it's new, and exploring it takes energy and concentration. It is a journey of its own, and many of the ways of coping in the desert will be helpful in Canaan. Focusing on co-creating in the new place, on taking care of yourself physically and emotionally, asking for help, are ways of living as well as good desert survival skills.

∿ A Parable ∿

In her collection of wisdom stories from around the world, Margaret Silf re-tells the story of a stream that wanted to cross the desert. Flowing down from high mountains, the stream is accustomed to moving along at its own pace, unobstructed, until it reaches the edge of the desert one day. Try as it might, each time the stream thrusts itself out into the desert, the water dries up and disappears. But the stream is used to having its way, so it continues to think positively and keeps trying to cross the desert anyway.

Finally, the desert speaks to the stream:

> You won't be able to cross the desert using the old methods that worked for you further up the mountain. It is no use hurling yourself in the desert like that. You will never cross the sand like that. You will simply disappear, or turn into marshland. No, you must trust the wind to carry you across the desert. You must let yourself be carried.

The stream doesn't believe what the desert is telling her, and she argues with the desert. How could the wind possibly carry an entire stream across the desert? "I won't be the same stream that I am now," she tells the desert. The desert replies:

> You certainly won't be the same stream you are now if you fling yourself into the sand and turn into a marsh. But let the wind carry you across the desert, and the real heart of you, the essence of everything you truly are, will be born again on the other side, to flow a new course, to be a river that you can't even imagine from where you are standing right now.[10]

The river finally let itself be carried by the wind across the desert in the form of clouds to the top of a new mountain on the other side, where it began to flow toward home again in a new way, renewed.

May your own journey be as fruitful as the stream's. May you find it within yourself to trust that you are being carried someplace

For the LORD will comfort Zion; he will comfort all her waste places, and will make her wilderness like Eden, her desert like the garden of the LORD; joy and gladness will be found in her, thanksgiving and the voice of song.

—ISAIAH 51:3

extraordinary by the One who will never let you fall. May you find yourself in a new place, flowing freely someday, at home again in the world and renewed.

Resources

Broken Body, Healing Spirit: Lectio Divina and Living with Illness, Mary Earle (Harrisburg, Penn.: Morehouse Publishing, 2003) and *Beginning Again,* Mary Earle (Harrisburg, Penn.: Morehouse Publishing, 2004). Two books that are helpful to people who are trying to adjust spiritually to living with illness.

Healing Liturgies for the Seasons of Life, compiled by Abigail Rian Evans (Louisville, Ky.: Westminster John Knox Press, 2004). An extensive collection of rituals from a variety of primarily Christian denominations but with some interfaith materials as well.

Joy Is Our Banquet: Resources for Everyday Worship, Keri K. Wehlander (United Church Publishing House, Etobicoke, Ontario, Canada, 1996). An easy-to-use book of short rituals for important moments and transitions in life.

Little Pieces of Light . . . : Darkness and Personal Growth, Joyce Rupp (Mahwah, N.J.: Paulist Press, 1994). A brief and helpful guide to living with darkness during transitional times.

Praying Our Goodbyes, Joyce Rupp (Notre Dame, Ind.: Ave Maria Press, 1988). An excellent primer on praying the farewells of life, along with suggested rituals.

Transitions, William Bridges (Reading, Mass.: Addison-Wesley, 1980). An excellent overview of the psychology of living in transition.

When the Heart Waits, Sue Monk Kidd (San Francisco: HarperSanFrancisco, 1990). Kidd's narrative of a time of transition in her own life.

Notes

CHAPTER ONE: THE RESTLESS SEASON

1. William Bridges, *Transitions: Making Sense of Life's Changes* (Reading, Mass.: Addison-Wesley, 1980).

2. Anthony De Mello, *Taking Flight: A Book of Story Meditations* (New York: Image Books, 1988), p. 34.

3. I am a big fan of inclusive language that doesn't assign a gender to God and use it almost exclusively. Occasionally, however, the effort to avoid a male or female pronoun results in a sentence that is so convoluted that it's just not worth the effort.

4. John R. Claypool, *The Hopeful Heart* (Harrisburg, Penn.: Morehouse Publishing, 2003), p. 45.

5. Howard Thurman, *The Mood of Christmas* (Richmond, Ind.: Friends United Press, 1973), p. 23.

6. Anthony De Mello, *The Song of the Bird* (New York: Image Books, 1982), p. 66.

7. Benedicta Ward, trans., *The Sayings of the Desert Fathers* (Kalamazoo, Mich.: Cistercian Publications, 1975), p. 154.

8. I am grateful to Marcus Borg for this particular term, which came up in a conversation between us.

9. Matthew Linn, Sheila Fabricant, and Dennis Linn, *Healing the Eight Stages of Life*, (Mahwah, N.J.: Paulist Press, 1988), p. 137.

10. Sue Monk Kidd, *When the Heart Waits* (San Francisco: HarperSanFrancisco, 1990), p. 4.

11. Keri K. Wehlander, "A Turning Season," in *Circles of Grace: Worship and Prayer in the Everyday* (Etobicoke, Ontario, Canada: The United Church Publishing House, 1998), pp. 22–25.

CHAPTER TWO: RESTLESSNESS AND CREATIVITY

1. Sue Monk Kidd, *When the Heart Waits*, p. 13.

2. Thomas Merton, *New Seeds of Contemplation* (New York: New Directions, 1961), p. 32.

3. Margaret Silf, *One Hundred Wisdom Stories from Around the World* (Cleveland, Ohio: Pilgrim Press, 2003), pp. 157–158.

4. Terence E. Fretheim, *Exodus* (Louisville, Ky.: Westminster John Knox Press, 1991), p. 53.

5. Fretheim, *Exodus*, p. 68.

6. See my *Hearing with the Heart* (San Francisco: Jossey-Bass, 2003), Chapter Four.

7. Miriam Therese Winter, *Woman Wisdom: A Feminist Lectionary and Psalter, Women of the Hebrew Scriptures: Part One* (New York: Crossroad, 1991), p. 234.

8. Margery Williams, *The Velveteen Rabbit* (New York: Doubleday, n.d.), p. 17.

9. Williams, *The Velveteen Rabbit*, p. 18.

10. De Mello, *Taking Flight*, pp. 58–59.

11. Fretheim, *Exodus*, p. 271.

12. Linda Clader, *Voicing the Vision* (Harrisburg, Penn.: Morehouse Publishing, 2003), pp. 12–17.

13. Henri J. M. Nouwen, *Lifesigns: Intimacy, Fecundity, and Ecstasy in Christian Perspective* (New York: Doubleday), pp. 65–66.

14. The poem comes from *Christina Rossetti*, compiled by Jan Marsh (London: J. M. Dent, 1996), p. 57.

CHAPTER THREE: HELP!

1. Adapted from "The Collect for a Person in Trouble or Bereavement," The Book of Common Prayer 1979 (New York: Oxford University Press, 1979), p. 831.

2. Nora Gallagher, *Practicing Resurrection: A Memoir of Work, Doubt, Discernment, and Moments of Grace* (New York: Alfred A. Knopf, 2003), pp. 10–11.

3. Mary C. Earle, *Broken Body, Healing Spirit: Lectio Divina and Living with Illness* (Harrisburg, Penn.: Morehouse Publishing, 2003), p. 2.

4. Thomas Merton, *New Seeds of Contemplation* (New York: New Directions, 1961), p. 115.

5. Bill Williams, *Naked Before God: The Return of a Broken Disciple* (Harrisburg, Penn.: Morehouse Publishing, 1998), pp. 32–33.

6. De Mello, *Taking Flight: A Book of Story Meditations*, p. 63.

7. Bridges, *Transitions: Making Sense of Life's Changes*, p. 11.

8. Edward Hays, *The Ladder* (Leavenworth, Kans.: Forest of Peace Publishing, 1999), p. 139.

9. L. William Countryman, *Forgiven and Forgiving* (Harrisburg, Penn.: Morehouse Publishing, 1998), p. 33.

10. Benedicta Ward, trans., *The Sayings of the Desert Fathers: The Alphabetical Collection*, p. 74.

11. Spiritual directors can be found by consulting local clergy, retreat centers, or seminaries. You can also find help in locating a spiritual director near you from the Web site www.sdiworld.com, the site of Spiritual Directors International.

CHAPTER FOUR: EAT, SLEEP, BEND, AND STRETCH

1. Lauren F. Winner, *Mudhouse Sabbath* (Brewster, Mass.: Paraclete Press, 2003), p. 10.

2. Fretheim, *Exodus*, p. 85.

3. Fretheim, *Exodus*, p. 230.

4. Sue Bender, *Plain and Simple: A Woman's Journey to the Amish* (New York: HarperCollins, 1991), pp. 7–8.

5. Stephanie Paulsell, *Honoring the Body: Meditations on Christian Practice* (San Francisco: Jossey-Bass, 2002), p. 131.

6. Fretheim, *Exodus*, p. 184.

7. Winner, *Mudhouse Sabbath*, p. 21.

CHAPTER FIVE: ARE WE THERE YET?

1. Belden C. Lane, *The Solace of Fierce Landscapes: Exploring Desert and Mountain Spirituality* (New York: Oxford University Press, 1998), p. 98.

2. Lane, *The Solace of Fierce Landscapes: Exploring Desert and Mountain Spirituality,* pp. 94–95.

3. The Rev. Anne Kitch, personal e-mail, August 2004.

4. Winter, *WomanWisdom: A Feminist Lectionary and Psalter, Women of the Hebrew Scriptures: Part One,* p. 127.

5. Lane, *The Solace of Fierce Landscapes: Exploring Desert and Mountain Spirituality,* p. 5.

6. De Mello, *Song of the Bird,* p. 27.

7. Lane, *The Solace of Fierce Landscapes: Exploring Desert and Mountain Spirituality,* p. 84.

8. Ellen Raskin, *Nothing Ever Happens on My Block* (New York: Scholastic Book Services, 1966).

9. Kidd, *When the Heart Waits,* p. 94.

10. Bridges, *Transitions: Making Sense of Life's Changes,* p. 120.

11. Molly Wolf, *A Place Like Any Other: Sabbath Blessings* (New York: Image Books, 2000), p. 55.

12. Anne Morrow Lindbergh, *Gift from the Sea* (N.Y.: Pantheon Books, 1955), pp. 87–88.

13. Terry Waite, "Footfalls in Memory." In Teresa De Bertodano, comp., *Soul Searchers: An Anthology of Spiritual Journeys* (Grand Rapids, Mich.: William B. Erdmans Publishing, 2001), p. 173.

14. Joyce Rupp, *Praying Our Goodbyes* (Notre Dame, Ind.: Ave Maria Press, 1988), p. 125.

CHAPTER SIX: YOU PUT YOUR RIGHT FOOT IN, YOU PUT YOUR RIGHT FOOT OUT

1. Janet Morley, *All Desires Known* (Harrisburg, Penn.: Morehouse Publishing), p. 80.

2. Joyce Rupp, *Little Pieces of Light . . . : Darkness and Personal Growth* (New York: Paulist Press, 1994), pp. 9–10.

3. Adrienne Rich, *Diving into the Wreck: Poems 1971–72* (New York: Norton, 1973), p. 23.

4. Paraphrased from a story in Anthony De Mello, *The Song of the Bird* (New York: Doubleday, 1984), p. 96.

5. Madeleine L'Engle, *Walking on Water* (Colorado Springs, Colo.: Waterbrook Press, 1980), p. 10.

6. Paraphrased from a story in Margaret Silf, *One Hundred Wisdom Stories from Around the World* (Cleveland, Ohio: The Pilgrim Press, 2003), pp. 80–81.

7. Henri J. M. Nouwen, *Lifesigns: Intimacy, Fecundity, and Ecstasy in Christian Perspective*, p. 34.

8. Esther de Waal, *Every Earthly Blessing: Rediscovering the Celtic Tradition* (Harrisburg, Penn.: Morehouse Publishing, 1991), p. 39.

9. De Waal, *Every Earthly Blessing: Recovering the Celtic Tradition*, p. 43.

10. Winter, *WomanWisdom: A Feminist Lectionary and Psalter, Women of the Hebrew Scriptures: Part One*, p. 320.

11. Adapted from a story told in Margaret Silf, *One Hundred Wisdom Stories from Around the World*, pp. 16–17.

12. Rupp, *Little Pieces of Light*.

13. Rupp, *Praying Our Goodbyes*, p. 131.

14. Retelling of a story in Anthony De Mello, *Taking Flight: A Book of Story Meditations*, p. 17.

15. Edward Hays, *Prayers to a Domestic Church* (Leavenworth, Kans.: Forest of Peace Publishing, 1979), p. 63.

CHAPTER SEVEN: HOME AGAIN

1. Kidd, *When the Heart Waits*, pp. 176–177.

2. Kathleen Fischer and Thomas Hart, *A Counselor's Prayer Book* (Mahwah, N.J.: Paulist Press, 1994), p. 140.

3. Fischer and Hart, *A Counselor's Prayer Book*, p. 142.

4. Fischer and Hart, *A Counselor's Prayer Book*, p. 141.

5. Rupp, *Praying Our Goodbyes*, p. 93.

6. Murray Bodo, *The Place We Call Home: Spiritual Pilgrimage as a Path to God* (Brewster, Mass.: Paraclete Press, 2004), p. 25.

7. Joyce Rupp's book, *Praying Our Goodbyes,* has a collection of excellent and simple rituals that can help you if you're having trouble thinking of something appropriate. Another excellent resource is compiled by Abigail Rian Evans, *Healing Liturgies for the Seasons of Life.*

8. The Book of Common Prayer 1979, p. 292.

9. Silf, *One Hundred Wisdom Stories,* pp. 132–133.

10. Silf, *One Hundred Wisdom Stories,* pp. 23–24.

The Author

Debra K. Farrington is a wise writer, popular retreat leader and speaker, and publishing insider with a growing following. She is the publisher of Morehouse Publishing. She was manager of the Graduate Theological Union Bookstore in Berkeley, California, and has published in *Spirituality and Health*, *The Lutheran*, *Alive Now*, *Catholic Digest*, *U.S. Catholic*, *Publishers Weekly*, and other magazines and journals. This is her seventh book. You can find a list of Debra's speaking engagements and contact information for Debra at her website: www.debrafarrington.com.

Other Books of Interest

If you enjoyed this book,
you may be interested in these other
recent titles from Jossey-Bass and Wiley.

Learning to Hear with the Heart:
Meditations for Discerning God's Will
Debra K. Farrington
Cloth
ISBN: 0–7879–6716–5

"Debra Farrington's meditations remind us that anyone can learn to listen to God and would make anyone want to begin."
—Barbara Cawthorne Crafton, Episcopal priest, author, and spiritual director

As faithful Christians, it is important we hear, see, feel, and think with the heart, for it is through the heart that we attune ourselves to the Spirit and to what God wishes for each of us. *Learning to Hear with the Heart* written as a companion for your discernment journey invites you to spend thirty days listening for God's guidance not only for the big questions of your life but for everyday matters as well. Drawing on a wealth of stories, Scripture, prayer, and questions for reflection, author Debra Farrington encourages readers to be fuller and more joyful participants in discerning the shape and direction of their lives and in learning to live closer to God. Individuals and groups can use *Learning to Hear with the Heart* as a companion book to the author's earlier work *Hearing with the Heart* or as an individual, inspirational guide to the discernment process.

Debra K. Farrington an insightful writer and popular retreat leader is publisher of Morehouse Publishing and the former manager of the Graduate Theological Union Bookstore in Berkeley, California. Farrington is the author of *The Seasons of a Restless Heart* and *Hearing with the Heart* from Jossey-Bass and has written for a wide variety of publications including *Spirituality and Health, Catholic Digest, The Lutheran, Publishers Weekly, U.S. Catholic,* and many others.

**Hearing with the Heart:
A Gentle Guide to Discerning
God's Will for Your Life**
Debra K. Farrington
Cloth
ISBN: 0–7879–5959–6

"Wise, thoughtful, gentle, honest Debra Farrington is exactly the kind of companion we are hoping to find to travel with us on our journey home."

—Robert Benson, author, *The Game: One Man, Nine Innings—
A Love Affair with Baseball* and *Between the Dreaming
and the Coming True: The Road Home to God*

"Debra K. Farrington knows that finding what to do with our lives and making courageous and wise decisions at crucial turning points is a primary need faced by all of us. She offers invaluable guidelines in her highly readable, *Hearing with the Heart.*"

—Malcom Boyd, poet/writer in residence, Episcopal Cathedral Center of St. Paul, and author, *Are You Running with Me, Jesus?*

"The perfect handbook for anyone seeking a direction in life: practical information combined with grace-filled writing and a thorough explanation of the discernment process. Highly recommended reading for church discernment groups."

—Nora Gallagher, author, *Things Seen and Unseen: A Year Lived in Faith* and *Practicing Resurrection: A Memoir of Discernment*

Only through learning to hear with our hearts tuned closely to God can we discern how we should find our way through the crowded and confusing thickets of our lives. In *Hearing with the Heart,* popular writer and retreat leader Debra Farrington leads you through a gentle process for discovering how to invite God's presence into every aspect of your daily life. As you put these suggestions into practice you will find yourself opening more and more to God's infinite possibilities for you.

White China:
Finding the Divine in the Everyday
Molly Wolf
Foreword by Phyllis Tickle
Cloth
ISBN: 0–7879–6580–4

"White china" is Molly Wolf's personal short-hand for the kind of religious language and ideas that often seem abstract and daunting. Those of us who don't already know them are left to struggle in a landscape of abstraction and purity, intimidated and uncomfortable with our ability to handle them. We might mispronounce the words or use them wrongly, and then what would people think of us? They're pure white china—we might get them dirty. We might drop and break them. And they certainly aren't something we can consume—who can eat china?

In this beautifully written collection of essays, Wolf takes the language of Christian faith and religion, sets it in the context of her keen observations of everyday experience, and unpacks it, opening it up to make it real and close up and important. This charming, quirky, and highly personal book is for those who yearn to be touched, to find meaning, and to deepen their faith through fresh literary explorations of the places where faith meets life.

Molly Wolf (Kingston, Ontario) is the founder of the Web site SabbathBlessings.com and author of *Hiding in Plain Sight; A Place Like Any Other; Angels and Dragons: On Sorrow, God, and Healing;* and *Knitlit* and *Knitlit (Too),* both with Linda Roghaar.

A Hidden Wholeness:
The Journey Toward an Undivided Life

Parker J. Palmer

Hardcover

ISBN: 0–7879–7100–6

A BookSense Pick, September 2004

"This book is a treasure—an inspiring, useful blueprint for building safe places where people can commit to 'act in every situation in ways that honor the soul.'"

—*Publishers Weekly*

"The soul is generous: it takes in the needs of the world. The soul is wise: it suffers without shutting down. The soul is hopeful: it engages the world in ways that keep opening our hearts. The soul is creative: it finds its way between realities that might defeat us and fantasies that are mere escapes. All we need to do is to bring down the wall that separates us from our own souls and deprives the world of the soul's regenerative powers."

—From *A Hidden Wholeness*

At a time when many of us seek ways of working and living that are more resonant with our souls, *A Hidden Wholeness* offers insight into our condition and guidance for finding what we seek—within ourselves and with each other.

Parker J. Palmer is a highly respected writer, lecturer, teacher, and activist. His work speaks deeply to people from many walks of life, including public schools, colleges and universities, religious institutions, corporations, foundations, and grass-roots organizations. The Leadership Project, a 1998 survey of 10,000 American educators, named him one of the thirty most influential senior leaders in higher education and one of ten key "agenda-setters" of the past decade. Author of six previous books—including the best-sellers *Let Your Life Speak* and *The Courage to Teach*—his writing has been recognized with eight honorary doctorates and several national awards. He holds a Ph.D. from the University of California at Berkeley and lives in Madison, Wisconsin.

**Finding Our Way Home:
Turning Back to What Matters Most**
Mark R. McMinn
Cloth
ISBN: 0–7879–7531–1

"In some quarters, Christians have a reputation for being deathly afraid of diversity, conflict, humor, sexuality, and most of the other things that help make life worth living. Here is a book to prove it need not be so. Mark McMinn writes honestly, movingly, and well from his rich immersion in life, exploring experiences we can all identify with and finding the dimension of depth hidden in them. He helps us to understand the enlivening and liberating meaning of 'the Word became flesh and dwelt among us, full of grace and truth.'"

—Parker J. Palmer, author of *A Hidden Wholeness,*
Let Your Life Speak, and *The Courage to Teach.*

"We are all caught within the confusing and contradictory swirl of emotions like love and hate, hope and despair, remembering and forgetfulness, loathing and longing. Mark McMinn pointedly reveals that what so ruthlessly and lovingly draws them all together is the deep gravitational pull of home."

—Michael Card, musician and author of
A Fragile Stone and *Scribbling in the Sand*

Written in an intimate, personal style, *Finding Our Way Home* draws on the powerful insights of psychology, Christian spirituality, and theology to explore the human longing for a home, a spiritual as much as a physical place where we are at peace with ourselves and with God. McMinn asks readers to consider the different aspects of home as a spiritual metaphor—what we grew up in as well as the challenges of living well within our present realities—and in the process he addresses the yearning for a spiritual center, a deeper relationship with God, and peace in our lives.

Mark McMinn (Winfield, IL) is Rech Professor of Psychology at Wheaton College where he also initiated and directs the Center for Church-Psychology Collaboration. He has authored over 100 journal articles and chapters and seven books, including *Why Sin Matters* (Tyndale, 2004).

**So Much More:
An Invitation to Christian Spirituality**
Debra Rienstra
Cloth
ISBN: 0–7879–6887–0

"So Much More is a radiant manifesto for the fully realized Christian life. Rienstra speaks to the heart without mawkishness, speaks to the mind without logic-chopping, and speaks to the doubtful without patronizing. With good humor, and with erudition worn lightly, Rienstra provides a compelling Christian account of sin and grace, reason and revelation, the longing for God, the mystery of suffering, and the pathways of love and service."

—Carol Zaleski, professor of religion, Smith College

What does it truly mean to live as a Christian? This intimate, engaging, and beautifully written book speaks to the heart of Christian faith and experience rather than to any one branch or theological position. Debra Rienstra weaves her own experiences as a Christian into chapters on central topics such as transcendence, prayer, churchgoing, the Bible, sin and salvation, and suffering. This is a book for people who don't have all the answers, those who are still thoughtfully considering the depth and breadth of their faith and would like an evocative and sympathetic companion to accompany them on their journey.

Debra Rienstra is a professor of English at Calvin College and the author of *Great with Child: Reflections on Faith, Fullness, and Becoming a Mother.* She lives in Grand Rapids, Michigan.

A World According to God:
Practices for Putting Faith at the
Center of Your Life
Martha Ellen Stortz
Foreword by Ron Hansen
Cloth
ISBN: 0–7879–5981–2

"Stortz's Christianity is devout yet not dogmatic, solidly based in Christian scripture yet
not narrowly so. Stortz's prose is often lyrical or
striking . . . fresh and profound."

—Publishers Weekly

"People are yearning to find life that really is life. Martha Stortz's beautifully crafted book offers wisdom to address that yearning, showing how
Christian practices offer life-giving connections—to God, to the world,
and to other people. Her eloquent testimony is refreshing reading, and
more importantly it also points us to renewing living."
—Gregory Jones, dean and professor of theology,
Duke University Divinity School

Martha Ellen Stortz explores essential Christian practices of discipleship
such as baptism, prayer, communion, forgiveness, and fidelity to help
readers understand more deeply what it means to live in "a world according to God." The book makes the connections between Christian practices and the moral life in a way that will help believers retrieve both a
sense of the sacred and a commitment to the world, and that will
strengthen us so that we can live according to our most profound beliefs.
Filled with lively anecdotes and fresh interpretations—informed by solid
theological understanding—the book offers new insights into what it
means to put faith at the center of life.

Martha Ellen Stortz is professor of historical theology and ethics at
Pacific Lutheran Seminary, a branch of the Graduate Theological Union
in Berkeley, California. She is a layperson in the Evangelical Lutheran
Church in America and is widely respected for her speaking and teaching in the church. She is the author of *PastorPower: Power and Leadership
in Ministry.*

A Song to Sing, A Life to Live:
Reflections on Music as Spiritual Practice
Don Saliers, Emily Saliers
Hardcover
ISBN: 0–7879–6717–3

"The Indigo Girl and her father focus on the many dimensions of music in one's spiritual life."

—*Publishers Weekly*

Indigo Girl Emily Saliers and her father Don Saliers explore the many dimensions of music as it relates to our spiritual lives. Music is a central practice in most expressions of spirituality and faith—whether it's the Christian music of seeker services, traditional hymnody, liturgical chant and singing, or popular music ballads about the meaning of life. In this rich exploration of music across all these settings and styles, authors Don and Emily Saliers interweave their own stories as well as those of others to reveal the importance of music as spiritual practice and a force for good in our lives, looking at such topics as music and justice, music and grief, music and delight, and music and hope.

Don Saliers (Atlanta, GA) is professor of theology at Candler School of Theology at Emory University. **Emily Saliers** (Atlanta, GA) is a member of the Indigo Girls, an award-winning folk-rock duo known for their social activism.

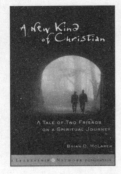

A New Kind of Christian:
A Tale of Two Friends on a Spiritual Journey
Brian D. McLaren
Hardcover
ISBN: 0-7879-5599-X

Winner of the *Christianity Today* Award of Merit
for Best Christian Living title, 2002!

"This is a book that heightens the depths and
deepens the peaks. Like all the best things in life,
it is not to be entered into lightly, but reverently and in the fear of a God
who is waiting for the church to stop asking WWJD, 'What would Jesus
do?,' and start asking WIJD, 'What is Jesus doing?'"
— Dr. Leonard Sweet, E. Stanley Jones Chair of Evangelism at
          Drew University, founder and president of
          SpiritVenture Ministries, and bestselling author

A New Kind of Christian's conversation between a pastor and his daughter's high school science teacher captures a new spirit of Christianity—
where personal, daily interaction with God is more important than
institutional church structures, where faith is more about a way of life
than a system of belief, where being authentically good is more important than being doctrinally "right," and where one's direction is more
important than one's present location. Brian McClaren reminds us that
this is but the beginning of the journey, and "whatever a new kind of
Christian is, no one is one yet . . . But every transformation has to start
somewhere." For all who are searching for a deeper life with God and a
more honest statement of authentic Christian faith, *A New Kind of Christian* will open the way for an exciting spiritual adventure into new territory and new ways of believing, belonging, and becoming.

Brian D. McLaren, named by *Time* magazine as one of the twenty-five
most influential evangelicals, is the founding pastor of Cedar Ridge
Community Church in the Washington-Baltimore area and the author
of acclaimed books on contemporary Christianity, including *The Story
We Find Ourselves In* and *The Last Word and the Word After That.*

Reimagining Christianity: Reconnect Your Spirit Without Disconnecting Your Mind
Alan Jones
Cloth
ISBN: 0–471–45707–8

"From his pulpit at Grace Cathedral in San Francisco, Alan Jones has influenced for good an entire continent of struggling Christians. In this provoking and helpful new book, he extends his voice to those both within and beyond the Church. A thinking Christian in a thoughtless world is what he is and what he aims to make us. This is a very good start."

— The Reverend Professor Peter J. Gomes, The Memorial Church, Harvard University, and author of *The Good Book*

"Here is a book for all who suspect that God is greater than religion, who regard imagination as a spiritual path, and who could use a wise companion on the way."

— The Rev. Dr. Barbara Brown Taylor, Episcopal priest, author, teacher, and lecturer

In this provocative new book, the internationally renowned Dean of the Episcopal Grace Cathedral in San Francisco delivers a resonant and comforting message to anyone looking for spiritual solace in today's troubled world. Dr. Jones inspires you to think, to question, to dig deeper into the truths of existence as a way of deepening your spirituality rather than accepting rigid dogma. Drawing on his vast knowledge of history, religion, and the heart, Jones encourages you to open doors to those of all faiths and even to those who profess no faith at all. As you do so, you can better understand the powerful promise of Christianity.

Alan Jones, Ph.D., is an Episcopal priest and the dean of Grace Cathedral in San Francisco, California. He lectures all over the world as well as on the Webby Award–nominated gracecathedral.org. Dr. Jones's books include *Seasons of Grace: The Life-Giving Practice of Gratitude,* winner of the prestigious 2004 Nautilus Award in the spirituality category.